J. Bruce Lindeman, Ph.D.
Professor, Department of
  Economics and Finance
University of Arkansas at
  Little Rock

Microeconomics

All inquiries should be addressed to:
Barron's Educational Series, Inc.
250 Wireless Boulevard
Hauppauge, New York 11788

Library of Congress Catalog Card No. 91-7785

International Standard Book No. 0-8120-4601-3

Library of Congress Cataloging-in-Publication Data
Lindeman, Bruce.
   Study keys to microeconomics / by Bruce Lindeman.
      p.   cm.
   Includes index.
   ISBN 0-8120-4601-3
   1. Microeconomics. I. Title.
HB172.L718   1991
339—dc20   91-7785
                                                          CIP

PRINTED IN THE UNITED STATES OF AMERICA

1234   5500   987654321

CONTENTS

Theme 1 INTRODUCTION TO MICROECONOMICS AND STUDY KEYS

*T*his Theme introduces the Study Keys and describes some of the fundamental objectives and elements of the study of economics. Study Keys should be used with your day-to-day study, to prepare for lectures and, especially, examinations. Each Study Key discusses a specific topic in Microeconomics and provides you with a short, point-by-point preview and review of the important subject matter that you will be learning in your course. Themes organize related Keys into broader topic areas.

Economics is the study of the manner in which society chooses to efficiently allocate its scarce resources. The study of economics has two general categories. Microeconomics studies the ways that firms and households make economic decisions. Macroeconomics examines the economy as a whole and the impact of government's activities and decisions.

INDIVIDUAL KEYS IN THIS THEME

1	Using the Study Keys
2	Objectives of economics
3	The market and allocation
4	Micro- and macroeconomics
5	Private and public sectors
6	Economic systems
7	Economic policy

Key 1   Using the Study Keys

OVERVIEW *This Key explains the purpose of this book and tells you how best to use it. Be sure to read this Key before using the book.*

Themes and Keys: This book contains 12 *Themes* and 111 *Study Keys.*
- Each Study Key discusses a specific topic in microeconomics.
- Themes organize related Keys into broader topic areas.

What to expect from the Study Keys: The Study Keys in this book have been designed to be used for a one-semester introductory course in microeconomics or to help you with the microeconomics content of a single course in general economics.
- They help you to understand the *basic ideas* in each of the topics they discuss.
- They contain the *essence* of each topic area. Therefore, Study Keys are short and to the point.
- They do not contain elaborate description and lots of examples.
- Study Keys hone in on recognized problem areas that students of microeconomics run into.
- Use the Study Keys with your textbook and lecture notes. Don't expect to get everything you need in the course from this book alone.

Day-to-day study: As you do your daily study, you can help yourself by using the Study Keys like this:
- Before you read about the various topic areas in your text, read relevant Study Keys. This preview will make it easier to understand what you read in your text.
- Do the same before each class. A few minutes with the appropriate Study Keys just before class will help you to understand better what your instructor lectures about.
- After classes or after reading assignments in your text, review the appropriate Study Keys. This will help you to organize the subject matter in your mind and to understand how the topics relate to one another.

Preparing for examinations: The Study Keys will be especially useful when you study for examinations.

- They contain the "meat" of the subject matter, the essential knowledge in microeconomics that you must learn.
- Because the Study Keys are short and to the point, a short time spent with them can help you to nail down the major ideas and concepts that probably will figure heavily in the examination.
- Use them to review topic areas you are having trouble with.
- They provide quick and *to-the-point* review of essential subjects. You don't have to search through a 1000-page book or pages and pages of notes to find discussion of critical points.

Features of the Study Keys: The Study Keys have a number of features you will find useful.

- *Overview*: Just like this introductory Key, each of the Study Keys starts with an *overview*, a summary of the Key's contents.
- *List of Assumptions*: There is a lot of theoretical discussion in microeconomics. As described in Key 10, many simplifying assumptions are used in these discussions, and it is important to keep track of them. These assumptions are described in Keys 11 and 12. Following the overview will be a list of assumptions used in that Key, when necessary. Remember, as you read a Study Key, that if it has a list like this one, the assumptions in the list apply to the discussion in the Key:

  Assumptions (Keys 10–12): *List of assumptions follows*

- *Diagrams and Graphs*: Microeconomics makes use of a lot of diagrams and graphs. Important ones that you'll encounter are illustrated and described in Study Keys.
- *Warnings*: Just as in any subject, economics has its little pitfalls where a student may go wrong or make mistakes. The Study Keys point out these trouble spots to you, so that you can be aware of them and make sure that you don't get tripped up.
- *References to other Study Keys*: Much of the subject matter in microeconomics builds upon what has been presented earlier in the course. Therefore, many Study Keys expect you to know material which was presented in other Keys earlier in the book. If so, they include references to the Keys that contain the information needed. Also, you will sometimes see references to later Keys in which further elaboration of the discussion occurs.

Key 2   Objectives of economics

OVERVIEW *Economics is the study of the way society makes choices in the allocation of scarce resources. In particular, economics studies the ways in which economic decisions are and can be made efficiently.*

Economics: Economics studies the manner in which people and societies *choose* to allocate the use of the *scarce resources* they have available, so as to produce goods and services.

Scarce resources: *Scarce* resources are those that are not abundant enough for everyone to be able to use all they want or need. They include *land*, *labor*, and *capital goods*. They are provided by nature (land, labor) and by investment made by previous and current generations (capital goods, training and education of labor, improvement of land).

Choice: Since resources are scarce, society must choose how to allocate them. A central theme of economics is the manner in which these economic choices are made, both by the society as a whole and by the consumers and producers who make up the economy.

Specialization and exchange: The major theme of microeconomics is the study of how specialized resources are allocated and how the product of each is exchanged for products of others.
* Individual resources can't be put to every kind of use. Each one is better at some things than at others. This means that resources *specialize*. In modern economies, specialization by resources is very much the rule.
* *Exchange* is a result of specialization. Specialized resources produce what they are best at and exchange some of their product for the things that are best produced by others.

Efficiency: Another important theme in economics is *efficiency*. In the economic sense, efficiency means the use of resources in what the society thinks is the most productive way.
* Specialization allows individual resources to be more productive. In economic terms, that means more efficient.
* At the level of the economy as a whole, efficiency means the allocation of resources to the uses that lead to the most desirable (to the society) collection of outputs.

4

Key 3   The market and allocation

OVERVIEW *The market is the "arena" of economics in which the exchange of goods and services occurs. In its pure sense, the function of the market is to allocate scarce resources. It does so by establishing prices for all goods, services, and resources.*

The allocation problem: Economists say "wants are unlimited, resources are scarce." The problem in the economy, then, is to distribute (allocate) a quantity of resources that falls far short of what is wanted. Allocation determines *what* is produced, *how* it is produced, and *who* gets it. Key 6 describes various economic systems that humankind has devised during its history in order to solve the allocation problem.

Markets: Most economic systems end up relying, in some way, upon markets. The function of a market is to allocate resources by equating *quantity supplied* and *quantity demanded* (discussed in detail in Theme 4).
- *Supply* refers to the quantity of a good or service that its producers offer for sale at different possible prices.
- *Demand* refers to the quantity of that good or service that those who want it are willing to buy at different possible prices.

Price: *Price* is the mechanism used in the market to equate quantity supplied and quantity demanded; the objective of markets is to reach a state in which the quantity producers are willing to supply and the quantity buyers are willing to buy are *equal, at the same price.*

Free goods: Some things *aren't* scarce, because there is more of them available at a price of *zero* (free) than the total of what everyone together wants. These are called *free goods*. They aren't "scarce," in the economic sense. They don't have to be allocated and aren't distributed by markets.
- Some desirable "goods," such as air, are so abundant that they are free goods (*clean* air is another story: see Key 100).
- Some things are free goods because practically nobody wants them: cancer, crabgrass.

Key 4   Micro- and macroeconomics

OVERVIEW *Microeconomics studies the individual elements of the economy: the firm (producer), the household (consumer), and the economic forces (public and private) that motivate their actions. Macroeconomics studies the economy as a whole, examining how economy-wide forces interact and how public policy affects the overall economy.*

Microeconomics: Microeconomics studies the individual decision makers in the economy and the motives behind their economic actions and decisions. It studies how producers, or *entrepreneurs and firms* (Key 16), and consumers, or *households* (Key 17), interact with one another in *markets*.
- Firms *produce* and sell goods and services. Microeconomics studies how firms decide what to produce, what resources to use to produce it, and how much of it to produce.
- Households *consume* (buy) goods and services from firms. Microeconomics studies how households allocate (budget) their limited incomes among the goods and services they desire and how they choose the selections of goods and services they will consume.
- Firms also can act as "consumers" when they consume raw materials, labor, and capital (Theme 10).
- Households also can act as "producers" when they provide labor to firms.

Macroeconomics: Macroeconomics examines the overall economy, rather than its individual elements. It studies aggregate national output, or national product, and examines the economy-wide forces that affect the level of output. Macroeconomics also studies the monetary system, overall price levels and changes (inflation and deflation), and the effects of government's expenditures, taxation, and borrowing upon the economy.

Key 5 Private and public sectors

OVERVIEW *One of the ways in which economists view the economy is to divide it into the private sector and the public sector. The private sector is made up of households and firms—private individuals and organizations that make their own economic decisions. The public sector is government and its activity and economic choices: taxation, choices concerning how government funds are spent, and the level of government control and regulation in the economy.*

The private sector: The private sector is made up of *firms* (Key 16) and *households* (Key 17). These private sector elements make their own economic decisions. They are influenced by their own private views of the markets they operate in and by their own needs and desires, and their economic ability to satisfy them.
- Firms make decisions concerning the use of resources to *produce output*: goods and services (Themes 7, 8, 9, 10).
- Households make *consumption* decisions: what to consume, how much of it to consume (Theme 6).
- Although they make their decisions themselves, firms and households are influenced by the operations of the markets in which they participate.

The public sector: The public sector is the economic activity of *government* (Themes 11, 12). Government secures most of its income through *taxes* of various kinds, though some of its income comes from other sources. Government makes decisions about the services and facilities it provides and pays for.
- Allocation of *public goods* (Keys 102, 103) is not necessarily influenced by markets, because some public goods cannot be allocated by market forces.
- The activity of government influences decisions made by individual firms and households.
- Taxation (Key 107) has effects upon households' incomes and profits of firms, and sometimes upon market prices.
- Government also *regulates* some economic activity (Keys 109, 110, 111).

Key 6   Economic systems

OVERVIEW *Various economic systems exist throughout the world or have been tried in times past. They differ in the extent to which the public sector dominates the economy and economic decision making.*

Economic systems: The different economic systems used throughout the world are distinguished by the degree to which government influences and controls economic activity.
- All claim to be the "best" mix of public and private sector activity: the one mix that best achieves the goal of economic efficiency.
- These claims are based largely upon beliefs and feelings that are not exclusively economic in nature. Rather, they are political, sociological, religious, cultural, etc.

The capitalist system: *Capitalism* or the *free-enterprise* system proposes private ownership of the means of production, with little interference from government. It recognizes that some goods and services are best provided by government but advocates the least amount of government activity that is reasonably possible.

The socialist system: *Socialism* proposes a more economically active role for government. It advocates a large set of governmental social programs (medical care, retirement, education, etc.) and government control of significant sectors of the economy (such as heavy industry, transportation, communications, utilities, etc.).

The centrally planned system: This system (practiced in Marxist countries) asserts that government allocates scarce resources more efficiently than the private sector or the market system. While it may allow some small-scale private sector activity, government owns most of the economy's significant production capacity.

The mixed-enterprise system: This is the system—a variety of capitalism—that prevails in the USA. The public sector is larger than the purely capitalist minimum, mostly in social programs. There is little direct government interference with private market transactions but some regulation of parts of the private sector, in the interest of maintaining economic growth, stability, and competition.

Key 7   Economic policy

OVERVIEW *Economic policy is the collection of activities that society, usually through government, undertakes in order to achieve the society's economic objectives. Economic policy recognizes that the "free market" forces of the real-world economy may not always have the results that society wants. The most common objectives of economic policy are efficiency, equity, redistribution of income and wealth, economic growth, and economic stability.*

Economic policy: The purpose of economic policy is to "rearrange" the society's economy differently from the way in which market forces would, if left on their own.
- Economic policy (Theme 12) usually is made and implemented by government.
- It can have a variety of objectives, all of which are supposed to make things "better" in some way.
- The judgment of what is "better" is a problem that is not really the province of economics, since it involves judgment based upon such noneconomic factors as fairness, morality, a society's beliefs, the notion of what is "right," etc.

Objectives of economic policy: Some more common objectives of economic policy are:
- *Efficiency*: Monopolies and industries with very few competitors tend not to allocate resources efficiently (Theme 9). Antitrust law and industry regulation attempt to restore efficiency (Keys 109, 110, 111).
- *Equity*: Much government activity in the economy is to assure that the economy operates more fairly. Assistance to the poor, the elderly, the handicapped, and small business are examples.
- *Redistribution of income and wealth*: As a part of equity, government also *redistributes* income and wealth among the population. Social security and welfare programs are examples.
- *Economic growth*: Growth (increased capacity to produce output) is seen as desirable, so government has policies designed to promote and stimulate economic growth.
- *Stability*: Government policies seek to promote and encourage a stable economic environment (low inflation, avoiding recessions, etc.).

Theme 2 THEORY AND MODELS
IN ECONOMICS

*L*ike other scientific investigation, economics follows scientific methods. One important aspect of science is the development of theories. Theories are attempts to explain the phenomena that are being observed, so as to provide a better understanding of them. Models are mathematical constructions that describe theoretical ideas. All theories and models contain simplifying assumptions, which help to make them less complicated and enable the scientist to zero in on the specific phenomenon being studied. A very important qualification for any theory or model is that it can be tested. In the hard sciences (physics, chemistry, etc.) it is possible to design laboratory experiments that can test theories. Economics, however, is a social science. It has no laboratories, so economists have to test their theories by using economic data from past history and by very careful observation of economic activity.

INDIVIDUAL KEYS IN THIS THEME

Key 8   Theory and models

OVERVIEW *Much of the study of economics is devoted to economic theories and economic models. Economists develop theories and models of what they think are the important forces that operate in the economy. These are examined in order to come to conclusions about economic forces and activity in the "real world."*

Theory and models: Theory exists in all scientific and investigative disciplines. It is an attempt to explain on paper how real-world phenomena are related. Models are the formal illustrations of theories. Often they are mathematical, but they don't have to be.

- Theory is abstract; it doesn't provide a complete picture of everything in the real world but is simplified so that we can study small chosen portions of it. Neither models nor theories must "look" exactly like the real world. The important thing is that they make *accurate predictions* about the real world.

- *Road map analogy*: Instructors often explain the usefulness of models with the example of a *road map*: a simplified model of the real-world system you use to get from one place to another by car. But 99 percent of the "real-world" things that you'd drive by (minor streets, buildings, stoplights, trees, etc.) aren't shown on the map, because they would just clutter it up with useless information that has nothing to do with choosing a travel route. Even so, road maps are quite useful.

Testing theory and models: It is a basic scientific premise that theory must be tested (and, therefore, testable) to determine if it can be relied upon as an explanation of real-world events. Key 9 discusses testing of economic theory and models.

- To test a theory, it is applied to real-world information to see if it can make predictions reliably.

- Discard theories that do not accurately predict the real world.

Economic theory and models: Much of economics is theory and models. Mathematical models, including graphs and formulas, are frequently used because they are easy to understand and are compact, easy to manipulate, and quick to show results.

- To keep the picture simple and manageable, most economic models contain *simplifying assumptions* (Key 10).

- Most of the *graphic illustrations* (Key 13) you will see in this or any other economics book are models.

Key 9   Testing economic theory

OVERVIEW *The scientific method requires that theories be tested in the real world; a good theory is one that consistently predicts the real world accurately. Economics has no laboratories, so scientific experiments cannot easily be made and variables are difficult to measure. Economics, therefore, relies heavily upon historical and current economic data in the testing of its theories.*

Testing theories and models: Theories must be tested in order to determine how well they predict the real world.
- Tests of theory must be *replicable*: this means that the test can be repeated by others and will yield the same results.
- Theories in hard sciences (chemistry, physics, etc.) can be tested in laboratories, under controlled conditions. This allows carefully designed experiments that make sure that the proper things are being tested under the proper conditions.

Testing economic theory: Economics deals with *human behavior*, which is hard to pin down or predict.
- Economics doesn't have laboratories where its theories can be tested. Economists can't force all or part of the economy to act in certain ways, or try certain things, in order to test a theory. They have to rely upon *observation* of the real world to get the information they need for testing their theories.
- Economists use *empirical* information—data of various kinds, showing how the economy and/or its parts perform or have performed in the past. These data aren't always accurate; also they can be vague or ambiguous. Information needed to test some economic theory just doesn't exist and must be constructed from whatever data does happen to be available.

Disagreement among economists: For these and other reasons, not all aspects of economic theory have been settled to the satisfaction of all economists. Much of the disagreement among them isn't as much about economic theory (what *can* be done) as it is about economic *policy* (the moral, political, etc., questions about what *should* be done). Decades ago the economist Milton Friedman coined the terms *positive* and *normative* economics. Positive economics studies economic forces and generally advocates little in the way of economic policy. Normative economics, however, is concerned with policy goals and achieving (usually by government action) them.

Key 10   Simplifying assumptions

OVERVIEW *Economic models contain simplifying assumptions, which strip away much real-world detail so that the model can concentrate upon the specific phenomena being studied. Students of economics must be very careful to recognize these assumptions and take them into account when making generalized conclusions about real-world economic activity.*

The purpose of simplifying assumptions: The real world is very complicated and elaborate in the way it works. Most scientific theories and models examine only a small part of the real world. They use *simplifying assumptions* to strip away much real-world detail that is not directly related to the phenomena being studied or that makes studying them very complicated.

Explicit assumptions: *Explicit assumptions* are those that are stated prominently in a model or theory, so that anyone examining it is easily aware of them.

Implicit assumptions: *Implicit assumptions* are *not* stated in a theory or model or are mentioned only obscurely. It is bad scientific practice to use implicit assumptions; all assumptions should be stated, even the most obvious ones.
- *Warning!* All scientific disciplines contain assumptions that are used so much that they often are implicit, because "everyone" knows about them. However, people who *aren't* familiar with the discipline can easily be misled.

Assumptions in economic theory: Many assumptions are commonly used throughout economic theory. Some important ones are described in Keys 11 and 12. Good economics textbooks carefully describe all the assumptions they use.
- *Warning!* Once your text has described assumptions, they might not be repeated as carefully in later discussion. However, *you* must remain aware of them at all times in order to properly understand what you are learning!
- *All Keys in this book that deal with economic theory will state the assumptions used!* Look for the list of assumptions just following the *Overview.*

Key 11   The *ceteris paribus* assumption

OVERVIEW *The* ceteris paribus *assumption is the most commonly used assumption in economics. It means "all else being equal." This assumption is often implicit; i.e., it is not specifically stated every time it is used.*

Note: *Ceteris paribus* is sometimes abbreviated *CetPar*.

Endogenous and exogenous variables: In a theory, *variables* are things that can *change*. These are what interest scientists the most, because they want to find out why the changes occur. *Endogenous* means "inside." Endogenous variables are those "inside" a theory or model: the variables that it is studying. *Exogenous* means "outside." Exogenous variables are all the *other* real-world variables that the theory is *not* studying.

***Ceteris paribus*:** *Ceteris paribus* is Latin for "all else being equal." The *ceteris paribus* assumption says that *none of the exogenous variables changes*. They ("all else") are "equal" (unchanging).
- The economic "real world" is very complex. It is difficult to study particular aspects of it, if we have to allow for all of the other things that are going on at the same time.
- *Ceteris paribus* simplifies such study by letting us ignore those other real-world details while we look at specific things.

Example: The theory of the firm (Themes 7, 8, 9, 10) examines the firm's operations and the forces motivating it.
- In reality nearly any decision made by a firm will have *some* impact in the rest of the world. Also, the world outside the firm is constantly changing, and that affects the firm.
- *Ceteris paribus* puts the world outside the firm "on hold" by saying that it stays the same (as far as the model is concerned).
- This lets us concentrate on what goes on *inside* the firm, without cluttering up our investigation with everything else that is going on everywhere else at the same time.

Warning! The *ceteris paribus* assumption is so common in economic theory that it often becomes implicit (not specifically stated in the discussion). Make sure *you* know when it is (and isn't) being used. Also, don't think that economic theory that uses *ceteris paribus* is always an accurate description of the real world. Remember, the function of *ceteris paribus* is to keep most of the complexity of the real world *out* of the theory.

Key 12   Other assumptions in economics

OVERVIEW *In addition to* ceteris paribus, *there are several other commonly used assumptions in economic theory.*

Warning! All these assumptions are common in economic theory. In some discussions they may be implicit (Key 10). You should make sure you know the assumptions behind what your instructor lectures about and what you read in your text. *When in doubt, ask your instructor.*

Note: Abbreviations for these assumptions shown in (parentheses) may be used in the assumptions lists in the Keys to save space.

The *efficient markets* assumption *(EffMar)*: This assumption states that economic markets operate in accord with the laws of economics, with perfect information (see below), and that no elements within the market make obvious errors. It assumes that changes in market conditions (demand, supply, prices, etc.) are instantly communicated to all economic elements, which then can react to them very quickly.

The *economic man* assumption *(EcMan)*: This assumption states that everyone in the market (men and women) act as *economic men.* They always act *rationally*, with the goal of *maximizing* their own *profits* or *utility* (satisfaction from consumption or other activity). They do nothing *irrational* (anything they know to be stupid, unprofitable, or otherwise conflicting with the economic goals of *maximizing profit and/or utility*).

Other common assumptions in economics: All of these, while unrealistic, are used to simplify models so that the particular economic forces being studied can be examined more clearly.
- The *perfect information* assumption (*PerfInfo*): Economic elements (firms and households) have immediate access to all necessary information that they need. They don't have to guess about what is going on in the markets in which they operate.
- The *costless* assumption (*Costless*): There are no costs of transportation, of obtaining knowledge, of shifting resources to different uses, of moving or changing the skills and other uses of labor, etc.
- The *instantaneous activity* assumption (*Instant*): Resources of all kinds can be shifted from one use to another at once, with no time spent doing so.

Key 13   Using graphs in economics

OVERVIEW *Most economic models are presented in mathematical form, usually as graphs and diagrams. These illustrations let us see a lot in a small space and are used to clarify and explain phenomena under study. In this Key, the use and understanding of graphs is explained.*

The nature of graphs: A graph is a picture that can be used to show many kinds of data and information, especially that which also appears in tables. Graphs are simpler to see and understand than tables, but it is harder to extract exact numbers from them.

The axes in a graph: The values of the variables in a graph are measured along the *axes*.
- The main side-to-side line is called the *horizontal axis*, or the *X-axis*, because variable X is measured along it.
- The main up-and-down line is called the *vertical axis*, or the *Y-axis*, because variable Y is measured along it.

The variables in a graph: *Variables* are the things that the graph measures and illustrates. This graph is *two-dimensional*, because it measures the relationship between *two* variables (X and Y).
- The variable measured on the vertical axis (or *Y-axis*) is called the *Y-variable*. It has a value of 0 where it intersects the *X*-axis, and the value gets higher going up the *Y*-axis. Values below the *X*-axis are *negative* values for the Y variable.
- The other variable (X) is measured on the *horizontal* axis (the *X*-axis). Its value is 0 where it intersects the *Y*-axis. To the right values get higher; to the left of the *Y*-axis, X is negative.
- X and Y can be any two different things for which one wishes to demonstrate a relationship; however, to show them on a graph, both X and Y *must* be things that can be expressed in *numbers*.

The illustrated graph: Many graphs used in microeconomics are set up like the one illustrated in this Key.
- In this graph, the X variable is *Quantity* (Q) and the Y variable is *Price* (P).
- In microeconomics, graphs like this one, with Price on the *Y*-axis and Quantity on the *X*-axis, are very often used.
- "Inside" the illustrated graph are two lines that cross: DD and SS. In this example, DD refers to *Demand* and SS refers to *Supply*.

- This is the same graph that is generated and discussed in Keys 25 through 31. Refer to those Keys for detailed descriptions of how this graph is derived and what it is showing.
- Line DD moves downward from the upper left to the lower right. It has *negative slope*.
- Line SS moves upward from left to right. It has *positive slope*.

KEY GRAPH

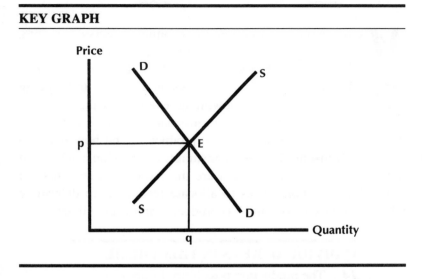

Interpreting a graph: The two lines show different relationships between price and quantity.
- Line DD shows how consumers react to changes in market price. They buy less at high prices and more at low prices. Each point on the line shows a combination of Price and Quantity; as one increases, the other decreases (showing a *negative*, or *inverse*, mathematical relationship).
- Line SS shows how producers react to changes in the price their product brings in the market. They produce more when prices are high and less when prices are low. Each point on the line shows a combination of price and quantity; they increase or decrease together (showing a *positive*, or *direct*, mathematical relationship).
- The two lines intersect at point E. At this point both lines show the same price (p) and same quantity (q).

Theme 3   BASIC CONCEPTS
IN ECONOMICS

*M*icroeconomics examines the economic decision-making processes of its important elements: firms and households. The production possibility frontier (PPF) often is introduced early in the study of microeconomics as a way of introducing graphs and models and of showing an example of the decisions required to allocate resources. Firms make decisions about production: what to produce, how to produce it, and how much to produce. Households make consumption decisions: what and how much to consume. Prices are the rationing device that an unregulated economy uses to allocate resources: to determine what is produced, how much is produced, and who will get it.

INDIVIDUAL KEYS IN THIS THEME

Key 14 The production possibility frontier

OVERVIEW *The production possibility frontier usually is the first graph introduced in the study of economics texts. It uses a simplified two-good model to describe how economic choices are made. It also demonstrates scarcity, choice, efficiency, and opportunity cost.*

Assumptions (Keys 10–12): *Ceteris paribus*

The production possibility frontier (PPF): The PPF is an economic model. It considers a society that can produce only two goods. We will call them *guns* and *butter*. (Note that this model has a very important simplifying assumption: the society produces only two goods. This assumption is unrealistic, but it lets us examine something important: deciding among economic alternatives so as to allocate resources efficiently.)

KEY GRAPH

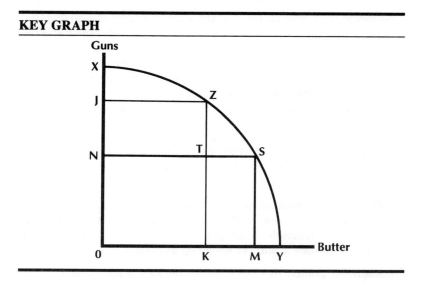

What the PPF demonstrates: There is a limited amount of resources available (*scarcity*, Key 2), so there are limits to the total amounts of guns and butter together that can be produced using them. The PPF shows the different combinations of gun and butter production that will most efficiently use the available resources.

• *Important*: resources used to produce one of the goods can't be used at the same time to produce the other.

- At point X, all resources are being used to produce the quantity X of guns, and no butter is produced. At point Y, all resources are being used to produce quantity Y of butter, and no guns are produced. At points *between* X and Y on the PPF some guns and some butter are being produced. *Example:* At point Z, the amount of guns produced is J, and the amount of butter produced is K.

Interpreting the PPF: The PPF usually is shown as a curved line, because some of society's resources are better at producing one of the goods than the other.
- Moving from close to the ends of the PPF (near X or Y) toward the middle yields large amounts of one good in return for giving up little of the other. This is because resources that are not very good at producing one good can be given up to the other, which they can produce more efficiently.
- At points closer to the middle of the curve (such as Z) resources that are better at producing one of the goods can more easily specialize. Compared to points near X or Y, more of one good must be given up to get a given quantity of the other.

Efficiency: All points on the PPF are *technically* efficient, in that for a given quantity of one good, the maximum amount possible of the other is produced. Moving *along the PPF* is the most *efficient* way to give up some of one good to get more of the other.
- *Example*: Moving from point Z to get more butter means that some guns have to be given up (*opportunity cost*, Key 18). If the society wants quantity KM *more* of butter, then according to the PPF, the quantity JN is the *least* possible amount of guns that could be "spent" to get the additional quantity KM of butter.
- Of all the points on the PPF, the one that best satisfies the society is the *allocatively* efficient point. We can't tell from the PPF alone which one that is (see Key 53).

Inefficiency: Any point *inside* the PPF is *inefficient*. From these points the society could get more of one of the goods without giving up *any* of the other. *Example*: From point T, production of guns could be increased to point Z without giving up *any* butter.

Unattainable points: Any point *outside* the PPF is *unattainable*. There are not enough *scarce* resources to produce the total quantities of guns and butter together that such points represent. *Example*: At point Z the society produces J amount of guns. It cannot, then, produce any more butter than amount K, which will require using *all* of the scarce resources it has available.

Key 15   The concept of the margin

OVERVIEW *The concept of the margin is one that often is poorly understood by beginning economics students. Marginality is extremely important to the understanding of economic theory and models, especially in microeconomics. Economic science frequently involves the study of the marginal unit of production, consumption, revenue, etc., and the reactions of economic elements to it.*

Warning! The concept of the margin in economics often is a difficult one for students to grasp. Make sure you understand it!

The margin and marginal measures: In microeconomic theory, firms and households make decisions at the margin. Marginal analysis examines the results of small changes from the current situation. Some examples of marginal measures in economics are:
- *Marginal utility* (Key 41) is the additional satisfaction (utility) a consumer gets from consuming one more unit of a good.
- *Marginal cost* (Key 60) is the additional cost to a firm of increasing production by one more unit of output.
- *Marginal revenue* (Key 68) is the additional revenue that a firm will receive if it sells one more unit of output.
- *Marginal physical product* (Key 90) is the additional output that a firm can produce if it uses one more unit of input.

Example: We consider *marginal utility* here, but the reasoning would be similar for other marginal measures. (The discussion here is incomplete; marginal utility is discussed more fully in Theme 6.)
- Suppose a consumer eats three bananas a day, getting a certain amount of satisfaction (which economists call *total utility*) from consuming them. If the consumer eats a *fourth* banana per day, the *additional* utility that the *fourth* one provides is the *marginal utility of the fourth banana.*
- Total utility increases by this amount; the utility provided by the first three bananas *does not change.*

Important: Marginal measures usually are *not the same* amount for all units in the total quantity (Key 56: diminishing returns; Key 42: diminishing marginal utility). *Example*: Marginal utility of each successive unit of a good is expected to *decrease* as consumption of it increases. (You enjoy eating a banana more if you haven't had any than if you'd already eaten three that day.)

Key 16   The firm and entrepreneurship

OVERVIEW *The firm is the economic unit responsible for decisions concerning what to produce, how it is produced, and how much is produced. In economic theory, the person(s) making the firm's decisions is called the entrepreneur. The firm's decisions are influenced by conditions that exist in the markets for factors of production and in output markets. Firms operate on the principle of maximizing profits.*

The firm as producer: The firm is the economic element that produces output. All firms together determine the market supply (Key 23) of goods and services. The theory of the firm (Themes 7, 8, 9, 10) studies the economic forces that influence what they produce, how much they produce, and what combinations of resources are used to produce it.

Entrepreneurship: *Entrepreneur* is the name given by economists to the person (or people) responsible for operating a firm and making the decisions about what it does and how it does it.
- *Entrepreneurship* is the art and science of making such decisions and taking the risks involved in doing so.
- The return to entrepreneurship is *profit:* entrepreneurs seek profit as their incentive for performing their function.

Normal profit and economic profit (*Important!*): *Normal profit* is the minimum profit level needed to induce entrepreneurs to start up firms in an industry and to continue operating those firms.
- Normal profit is distinguished from *economic profit*, sometimes called *excess profit* (as discussed in Themes 8, 9). Economic profit is profit in excess of normal profit.
- Normal profit is a *necessary cost of production.*
- Firms will stay open if the market eliminates *economic profit.*
- If profit stays below the *normal profit* level, they may remain open in the short run, but in the long run they will close down (Key 73).

The firm as consumer: Firms also "consume." They buy factors of production (Key 88) in input markets (Theme 10): raw materials, equipment, labor, etc., which they combine in production.

The firm as a profit maximizer: Firms' decisions are based upon the principle of *profit maximization* (Key 69). The firm's goal is to arrange its operations so that it makes the highest possible profit from them.

Key 17 Households

OVERVIEW *In economic theory, households are the consuming elements in the economy. They allocate their limited incomes to the purchase of goods and services in order to satisfy their needs. Households operate on the principle of maximizing utility.*

Households as consumers: Households are the economy's *consumers.* Their collective action determines market *demand* (Key 20) for goods and services.
- Households buy goods and services from the firms that produce them.
- Household consumption decisions are based upon market forces that determine the prices of goods and services.

Households as producers: Although we view households as consumers, they also act as producers in that they provide and sell *labor*, which is one of the inputs (Key 88) used by firms.

Utility maximization: The economic goal of the household is to *maximize utility* (Theme 6).
- *Utility* (Key 41) is a measure of the satisfaction and enjoyment received from the consumption of goods and services.
- The household receives *utility* from the consumption of goods and services.
- To maximize utility, it will seek the one combination of goods and services it can afford to consume that yields the most utility (Keys 44, 50).

Income constraint: Households are *constrained by their incomes* (Keys 43, 50).
- They cannot buy any more goods and services than their incomes will allow them to pay for.
- Because its ability to consume is limited by its income, the household must determine its utility maximization by choosing the one "market basket" of goods and services that it can afford that will give it the highest utility.

Key 18   Opportunity cost

OVERVIEW *Opportunity cost is the trade-off that must be sustained when an economic choice is made. Specifically, it is the value of the next-best alternative that is forgone when an economic choice is made.*

Assumptions (Keys 10–12): *CetPar, EcMan*

The concept of opportunity cost: *Opportunity cost* is the economist's way of saying that nothing is really free. When you make a constrained choice (Key 44) to consume some amount of a particular good, you have less resources (income, time, etc.) to spend on everything else. The *opportunity* cost of any choice you make is the value of the next-best choice you could have made with the same resources.
- You make these choices every day. Choosing lasagna for dinner means you can't spend the same money (or the same appetite) on steak or anything else. The *opportunity cost* of the lasagna is the value, to you, of whatever you *didn't* choose.
- You also choose among non-money alternatives. When you go to a movie, the opportunity cost is not only the goods you could have bought with the ticket money but also the other things you could have done with the *time* you spent.

  When rational choices are made, opportunity cost always is *less* than the value of what is chosen. Choosing lasagna means you decided that the same money, time, etc., spent on anything else would not have given you as much utility (satisfaction) as the lasagna.

Opportunity cost and social choice: The production possibility frontier (Key 14) illustrates opportunity cost. To produce a certain amount of good A, the society must give up a certain amount of good B. The opportunity cost of that amount of A is the value to the society of the quantity of B that it has to forgo. Much of the political activity of government has to do with the choices that must be made about spending and taxation.
- *Example:* The opportunity cost of a tax is the value of whatever the society's firms and households could have produced and consumed if they hadn't had to pay the tax instead.
- *Example*: The opportunity cost of a government program is the value of whatever else government could have done with the money it cost: Raising social security benefits will mean that less can be spent on military, roads, or whatever.

Key 19   Money and price

OVERVIEW *Prices usually are expressed in money, which is any widely accepted medium of exchange. In a barter economy, goods and services are traded directly; the existence of money allows for easier exchange of goods and services. In free (unregulated) markets, prices are determined by interaction of supply and demand and perform the economic function of allocating scarce resources.*

Barter: In primitive economies (and sometimes even in advanced ones), goods and services are traded directly: Five bushels of wheat for one goat; your car for my stereo, refrigerator, and dog, etc.
- This type of direct trading is called *barter.*
- Successful barter requires *coincidence of wants: each* person must have, and be willing to exchange, something the other wants.

Money: In advanced economies there is little direct trading; instead, *money* is used as a *medium of exchange.*
- Money is used as a measure of value and for exchange.
- Money is anything that is commonly accepted within the economy as a medium of exchange; it can be precious metals, coin, bills printed by government, checks, credit card lines, etc.
- The advantage of money is that it provides a measure of the value (i.e., price) of everything in common terms.
- Coincidence of wants is *not* necessary when money is used. Instead of trading goods and services directly, people use money. They accept money in trade for their goods and services because they know that they can exchange that money with other people for goods and services.

Price and resource allocation: Price is used in unregulated economies as the mechanism that distributes scarce resources. It determines "who will get what": how resources will be distributed among producers and consumers and what the economy's mix of production will be.
- Price is determined by interaction of *supply* and *demand* (Theme 4). It is the economic mechanism that drives markets toward *equilibrium.*
- Price is used by consumers to measure their incomes and to allocate their incomes among available goods and services (Theme 6).
- Price is used by firms to determine their costs of inputs (Theme 7) and their equilibrium production levels (Themes 8, 9, 10).

Theme 4 SUPPLY AND DEMAND

Supply and demand are the forces that drive markets and are the fundamental aspects of microeconomics. Firms decide what to produce, how to produce it, and how much to produce; households decide what and how much to consume. Economic activities that determine society's allocation of its resources depend upon supply and demand. Market equilibrium is the result of the balance between the forces of supply and demand in the market. At equilibrium, quantity demanded and quantity supplied are the same, at the same price. When a market is in equilibrium, there is no economic force operating to change quantity supplied/demanded and price. Departure from equilibrium often occurs; then economic forces that cause the market to move toward equilibrium again come into play.

Note: C*etPar* applies throughout this Theme.

Key 20 Demand

OVERVIEW *Demand is one side of the well-known economic "equation" of supply and demand. Demand is the expression in the market of the cumulative willingness of all consumers to buy various amounts of product at various prices. The law of demand states that consumers buy less at high prices and more at lower prices.*

Assumptions (Keys 10–12): *Ceteris paribus*

Essentials of demand: Demand is an *economic* phenomenon.
- Demand does *not* reflect what households *want* or *need*; it reflects only what they are *willing and able to pay for*.
- Households are willing to buy different amounts of each good at different prices.
- *Market demand* is the sum of the demand of all households.

The law of demand: The *law of demand* is illustrated in the graph in Key 22. It states that quantity demanded (Q) will be low at high prices (P) and high at low prices.

The demand curve: Line DD in the graph is the *demand curve*.
- Even though the demand curve shown is a straight line, mathematicians call it a "curve." In economics texts, demand curves usually are shown as straight lines, though for many goods, "real world" demand curves could indeed be curved lines.
- Line DD in this graph represents *market demand* for a particular good. Market demand is *cumulative* demand—the added-up demand of *all* households taken together.
- The demand curve DD shows how much of the good (Q) households will buy in the market at each possible price (P).

Normal goods: Most goods are *normal goods*—their demand curves slope downward from left to right (negatively).

Giffen goods: There are some goods (called *Giffen goods*) that do not obey the law of demand. Their demand curves go the "wrong" way: quantity demanded is higher at high prices than at low prices. *Example*: Some exotic goods (weird pets, "prestige" brands of some goods, etc.) are desirable mainly *because* they are expensive; they are used to show off the owner's wealth but aren't much use for anything else. If they were cheap, they wouldn't serve this purpose, and the quantity demanded of them would be less.

Key 21   Demand schedules and functions

OVERVIEW *The demand curve depicts demand on a graph. Any graphical depiction can also be shown in a table or in a mathematical formula, called a function. In economics, a demand schedule is a table that shows the same information shown by a demand curve in a graph. A mathematical formula that explains demand is called a demand function.*

Assumptions (Keys 10 –12): *Ceteris paribus*

Demand curves, schedules, and functions: The graph in Key 22 shows a *demand curve*. The information shown by the curve also can be shown by a mathematical formula (*a demand function*) or in a table (*a demand schedule*).

Demand function: If you look at the numbers on the graph in Key 22, you will notice that as price increases by $4, quantity demanded falls by 100. This suggests a mathematical relationship between price and quantity demanded.
- Such a relationship is called a *demand function*. For the graph in Key 22, the demand function is:
$$Q = 450 - 25\ (P).$$
- *Example*: if P = $4, then the formula would be:
$$Q = 450 - 25\ (4) = 450 - 100 = 350$$

Demand schedule: The graph in Key 22 shows how quantity demanded is related to price. The prices and quantities shown on the graph can be shown in tables, called *demand schedules*. Two are shown below. The schedule on the left uses the numbers from the graph. The one on the right uses the demand function (above) to generate quantities for other prices, too. Both are equally valid.

Price	Q demanded	Price	Q demanded
		$ 4	350
		$ 6	300
$ 4	350	$ 8	250
$ 8	250	$10	200
$12	150	$12	150

Warning: Many economists use the term *demand function* to mean *demand curve*; this is a habit that mathematicians often have. However, you should keep the terms straight.

Key 22 Quantity demanded

OVERVIEW *Market demand (the demand curve) shows the amount of a good that all households together will buy at each different price. The amount of the good that all households together will buy in the market at a given price is called the quantity demanded at that price.*

Assumptions (Keys 10–12): *Ceteris paribus*

Quantity demanded: *Quantity demanded* is the amount of a good that will be purchased in the market at a given price. The graph shows different price and quantity demanded combinations.
- At market price P_1 ($8), quantity demanded is Q_1 (250 units).
- At market price P_2 ($12), quantity demanded is Q_2 (150 units).
- At market price P_3 ($4), quantity demanded is Q_3 (350 units).

Effects of changes in price: Suppose that price starts out at P_1, with associated quantity demanded of Q_1.
- If price *rises* from P_1 to P_2, quantity demanded will *fall* from Q_1 to Q_2: At higher prices, a lower quantity will be demanded.
- If price *falls* from P_1 to P_3, quantity demanded will *rise* from Q_1 to Q_3: At lower prices, quantity demanded will be higher.

KEY GRAPH

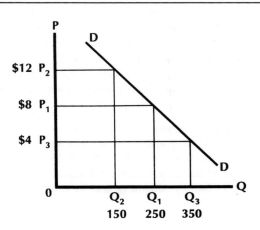

Key 23   Supply

OVERVIEW *Supply is one side of the well-known economic "equation" of supply and demand. Supply is the expression in the market of the cumulative willingness of all firms to produce various amounts of product at various prices. The law of supply states that firms will produce more at high prices and less at lower prices.*

Assumptions (Keys 10–12): *Ceteris paribus*

Essentials of supply: Firms produce goods (*output*). The amount they produce depends upon the market price they can get for the good(s) produced (Themes 8, 9).
- Not all firms produce every product.
- *Market supply* is the aggregate quantity (Q) of a good that all the firms that produce it will make available at all possible prices (P).

The law of supply: The *law of supply* is illustrated in the graph in Key 24. It states that quantity supplied (Q) will be low at low prices (P) and high at high prices.

The supply curve: Line SS in the graph is called the *supply curve*.
- For convenience, supply curves often are shown as straight lines, though mathematicians call them curves, just as for demand curves (Key 20).
- Line SS, in this graph, represents *market supply* for a particular good. It reflects the *cumulative supply* for all firms.
- The supply curve SS shows how much (Q) will be supplied by all firms in the market at each possible price (P).
- The supply curve in a graph usually slopes upward from left to right (positively). This reflects the law of supply. (For an exception, see Key 96.)

Supply schedules and supply functions: Just as with demand, it is possible to describe the supply curve's graphical information in a table (*a supply schedule*) or in a mathematical formula (*a supply function*). Refer to the explanation for demand schedules and functions in Key 21. Supply schedules and functions are obtained the same way.

Key 24   Quantity supplied

OVERVIEW *Market supply (the supply curve) shows the amount of a good that all firms together will produce at each different market price. The quantity of the good that all firms together will produce at a given price is called the quantity supplied at that price.*

Assumptions (Keys 10–12): *Ceteris paribus*

Quantity supplied: Quantity supplied is the amount of a good that firms will be willing to sell in the market at a given price. The graph below shows various price/quantity supplied combinations.
- At market price P_1, quantity supplied is Q_1.
- At market price P_2, quantity supplied is Q_2.
- At market price P_3, quantity supplied is Q_3.

Effects of changes in price: In the graph, assume that the market price is P_1. At that price, quantity supplied is Q_1.
- If price *falls* from P_1 to P_2, quantity supplied will *fall* from Q_1 to Q_2. At lower prices, a lower quantity will be supplied.
- If price *rises* from P_1 to P_3, quantity supplied will *rise* from Q_1 to Q_3. At higher prices, quantity supplied will be higher.

KEY GRAPH

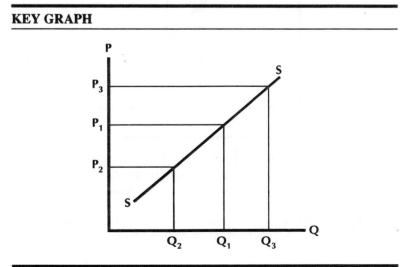

Key 25   Market equilibrium

OVERVIEW *Market equilibrium between supply and demand occurs at the one (and only) price at which quantity supplied and quantity demanded are equal. At equilibrium, there are no market forces operating to change quantity or price. Equilibrium is demonstrated in a graph by the intersection of the supply and demand curves.*

Assumptions (Keys 10–12): *Ceteris paribus*

Equilibrium: The intersection of the demand curve DD (Key 22) and the supply curve SS (Key 24), point E on the graph, demonstrates *equilibrium* between market supply and market demand.

KEY GRAPH

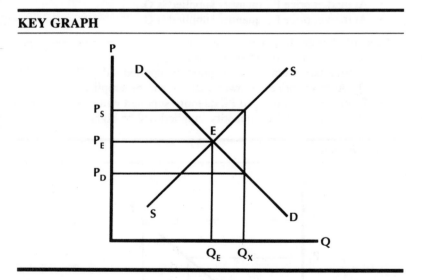

- The intersection of DD and SS is the only point on the graph where quantity demanded and quantity supplied are equal at *the same price*. This condition defines market equilibrium.
- So long as demand (DD) and supply (SS) do not change, the market will remain in this equilibrium and will be stable. (Keys 26–31 discuss what happens to market equilibrium when SS and DD *do* change.)

Key 26   Departure from equilibrium

OVERVIEW *Departure from equilibrium (disequilibrium) can occur for a variety of reasons. It creates an unstable situation in the market within which market forces operate to restore an equilibrium.*

Assumptions (Keys 10–12): except as noted, *CetPar*, *PerfInfo*

Disequilibrium: The graph in Key 25 shows a market in equilibrium. The supply and demand curves intersect at point E, where market price is P_E and market quantity demanded/supplied is Q_E.
- *Disequilibrium* occurs when the price prevailing in the market is *not* P_E. The discussion in Key 25 tells us that this also means that quantity demanded and quantity supplied are not the same either.
- Disequilibrium is an unstable situation. Keys 27–31 describe how market forces cause firms and households to act to restore a market equilibrium.

Departure from equilibrium: In a stable market that is in equilibrium, there are no forces that would cause a departure from equilibrium. In the "real world," however, many things can happen to cause an equilibrium to become unstable.
- *Important note:* If we're making the *ceteris paribus* assumption (Key 11), then disequilibrium occurs because something *exogenous* to the model happens. That is, "all else" in the real world doesn't "remain equal."
- *Shifts in demand* (Key 28) occur when something causes the demand curve to move to some other position. *Shifts in supply* (Key 29) occur when something causes the supply curve to move to another position.
- If the *perfect information assumption* (Key 12) is violated, then *misjudgment* by firms of actual market demand can lead them to produce nonequilibrium amounts of product.
- Regardless of the reason, if any deviation from equilibrium occurs, market forces will encourage the market to readjust itself toward equilibrium (Key 27).

Key 27   Restoring market equilibrium

OVERVIEW *Any time quantity supplied, quantity demanded, or price move away from their equilibrium levels, market forces will operate to restore an equilibrium. This means that anytime the market is not in equilibrium, market forces will act to move the market closer to equilibrium.*

Assumptions (Keys 10–12): *Ceteris paribus*, except for exogenous factors

---

KEY GRAPH 1

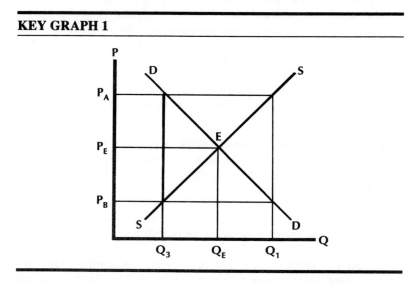

Excess supply: If firms produce more than the equilibrium quantity (Key 25), say quantity Q_1, and charge price P_A, there will be *surplus* (also called *excess supply*, or a *shortfall in demand*).

- At price P_A, quantity demanded is only Q_3, much less than Q_1.
- As a result, firms will have to cut back their production and reduce price to sell the surplus. By the law of demand (Key 20), the quantity demanded (Q_D) will rise as price falls. By the law of supply (Key 23) the quantity supplied (Q_S) will fall as price falls.
- This will continue until Q_S and Q_D both are equal (at quantity Q_E). This will be at the equilibrium point E, where price is P_E.

Excess demand: The same reasoning can be used if firms produce less than the equilibrium quantity, say quantity Q_2. A *shortage (excess demand* or *shortfall in supply)* will exist.

- If, for some reason, firms think equilibrium is at point S_X, they will charge price P_X, and produce quantity Q_2.
- At price P_X, quantity demanded is Q_4, which is much more than Q_2. This situation will encourage firms to increase price and increase production. By the law of demand (Key 20), the quantity demanded (Q_D) will fall as price rises. By the law of supply (Key 23) the quantity supplied (Q_S) will rise as price rises.
- This will continue until Q_S and Q_D both are equal (at quantity Q_E). This will be at the equilibrium point E, where price is P_E.

KEY GRAPH 2

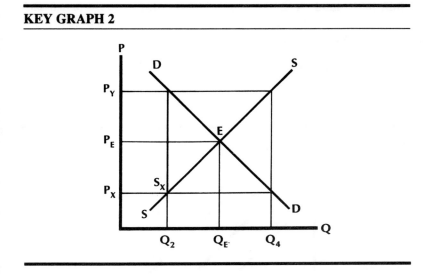

Key 28 Shifts/changes in demand

OVERVIEW *Demand in the market does not always stay the same. Prices change, and quantities change. If the demand curve changes its position, it is called a shift in demand. If the change is due to a shift in the supply curve, a change in quantity demanded will occur along the same demand curve.*

Assumptions (Keys 10–12): *Ceteris paribus* except as noted

Shift in demand: A *shift in demand* (also called a *change in demand*) occurs when the *entire* demand curve for the market moves to a different position. This means that for all prices, the quantity demanded now is different. The shift can be *outward* or *inward*. Both kinds are shown in the diagram below. (Effects upon supply are described in Key 30.)

Illustration: The original equilibrium (Key 25) demand curve is D_1.

KEY GRAPH

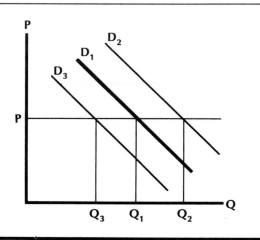

Outward shift in demand: The curve will shift outward if market demand *increases* (from curve D_1 to, say, curve D_2, so that quantity demanded at price P is now greater: it is now Q_2).

Inward shift in demand: The curve will shift inward if market demand decreases (from D_1 to, say, D_3 so that quantity demanded at price P is now less: it is now Q_3).

Why demand can shift: In the simple supply/demand model we've discussed up to now, *ceteris paribus* ignores exogenous variables (things that happen outside the model). Here are some common examples of exogenous, real-world causes of shifts in demand:
- *Changes in consumers' incomes*: If their incomes rise, they can afford more, and their demand for all kinds of goods and services increases (shifts outward). Conversely, then, if incomes fall, demand will decrease (shift inward).
- *Changes in tastes*: For various reasons (fads, new information, etc.), consumers may decide they like a certain good more (or less) than they used to. When this happens, demand increases (or decreases) and the curve shifts.
- *Change in the price of a substitute good* (Keys 44, 45, 50, 51): demand for a particular good may change if the price of a substitute for that good changes.

Change in quantity demanded: A shift in demand usually leads to a change in equilibrium price and equilibrium quantity demanded.
- The only time it won't is if the supply curve happens to shift at the same time in such a way that, by coincidence, the same price or the same quantity demanded/supplied exists at the new equilibrium.
- If only the *supply curve* shifts, then a change in equilibrium quantity demanded also will occur, but on the *same* demand curve as before (Key 31).

Warning! Make sure you understand the difference between a *shift in demand* (or *change in demand*) and a *change in quantity demanded*.
- A *shift in demand* (or *change in demand*) means that the market demand curve actually has *moved* to a *new* position.
- A change in *quantity demanded* means that there is a new equilibrium but *not necessarily* a new demand curve. A change in quantity demanded can occur on the *same* demand curve when only the *supply* curve shifts. (See Key 31 for effects of shifts in supply upon unchanging demand curves.)

Key 29   Shifts/changes in supply

OVERVIEW   *Supply in the market does not always stay the same. Prices change, and quantities change. If the supply curve changes its position, it is called a shift in supply. A change in quantity supplied (along the same supply curve) also occurs if the demand curve shifts.*

Assumptions (Keys 10–12): *Ceteris paribus* except as noted

Shift in supply: A *shift in supply* (also called a *change in supply*) occurs when the *entire* supply curve for the market moves to a different position. This means that for all prices, the quantity supplied now is different. The shift can be *outward* or *inward*. Both types of shifts are shown in the diagram. (Effects upon demand are shown in Key 31.)

Illustration: Assume that the original equilibrium supply curve is S_1.

KEY GRAPH

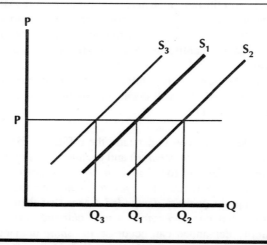

Outward shift in supply: The curve will shift outward if market supply *increases*. Shifting from curve S_1 to curve S_2 illustrates an outward shift in supply. A result of this shift is that quantity supplied at price P has increased: it is now Q_2.

Inward shift in supply: The curve will shift inward if market supply *decreases*. Shifting from curve S_1 to curve S_3 illustrates an inward shift in supply. A result of this shift is that quantity supplied at price P decreases: it is now Q_3.

Why supply curves shift: The discussion of shifts in demand (Key 28) points out that the *ceteris paribus* assumption allows the simple supply/demand model to ignore many real-world exogenous variables. In the discussion of the theory of the firm (Themes 7, 8, 9), many of these effects are considered. Some of these could cause a shift in supply.

* *Changes in factor prices* (prices of the things firms use in their production process): This is discussed in Theme 10.
* *Change in the number of firms in the industry* (Themes 8, 9): If new firms enter the industry, supply will increase; if existing firms close down, supply will decrease.
* *Change in structure of an industry* (Theme 9): Industries that have lots of small firms differ from those with few firms in the way supply is determined; sometimes growth and change in an industry can change its structure.
* *Technological change* (Keys 62, 63): New inventions, new ways of doing things, can affect an industry's market supply.

Change in quantity supplied: A shift in supply usually leads to a change in equilibrium price, and equilibrium quantity supplied.

* The only time it won't is if the demand curve happens to shift at the same time so that, by coincidence, the same price or the same quantity demanded/supplied exists at the new equilibrium.
* If only the *demand curve* shifts, then a change in quantity supplied will occur, but on the *same* supply curve as before.

Warning! Make sure you understand the difference between a *shift in supply* (or *change in supply*) and a *change in quantity supplied*.

* A *shift in supply* (or *change in supply*) means that the market supply curve has actually moved to a new position.
* A *change in quantity supplied* means that there is a new equilibrium but not necessarily a new supply curve.
* A change in quantity supplied can occur on the *same* supply curve if it is the *demand* curve that shifts. (Effects of shifts in demand upon unchanging supply curves are described in Key 30.)

Key 30 Demand shifts/quantity supplied

OVERVIEW *If the demand curve shifts, a new equilibrium will occur and a new quantity supplied will be determined. The change in quantity supplied occurs along the same supply curve. It is important to understand that since the supply curve remains the same, market supply has not changed (shifted). Only the quantity supplied changes.*

Assumptions (Keys 10–12): *Ceteris paribus*

Illustration: Shifts in demand along the same supply curve will result in new equilibrium positions, with both price and quantity demanded and supplied different from the original equilibrium E, where price is P_1 and quantity demanded/supplied is Q_1. Using supply curve SS in the diagram below:

KEY GRAPH

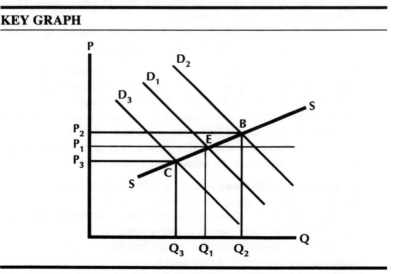

- *Outward shift in demand*: If the demand curve moves outward (D_1 to D_2), equilibrium moves along SS from E to B. Price is higher (P_2) and quantity demanded/supplied is higher (Q_2).
- *Inward shift in demand*: If the demand curve moves inward (D_1 to D_3), equilibrium moves along SS from E to C. Price is lower (P_3), and quantity demanded/supplied is lower (Q_3).
- In both cases, market equilibrium has changed but along the *same* supply curve.

Key 31   Supply shifts/quantity demanded

OVERVIEW *If the supply curve shifts, a new equilibrium and a new quantity demanded will be determined. The change in quantity demanded occurs along the same demand curve. It is important to understand that since the demand curve remains the same, market demand has not changed (shifted). Only the quantity demanded changes.*

Assumptions (Keys 10–12): *Ceteris paribus*

Illustration: The original equilibrium is at point E, where price is P_1 and quantity demanded/supplied is Q_1. Using demand curve DD in the diagram below:

KEY GRAPH

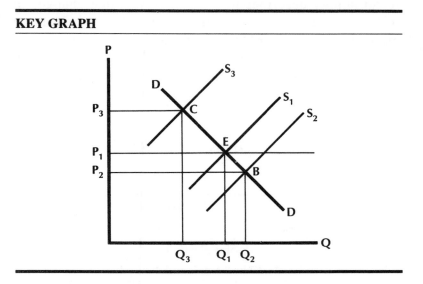

- *Outward shift in supply:* If the supply curve moves outward (S_1 to S_2), equilibrium moves along DD from E to B. Price is lower (P_2) and quantity demanded/supplied is higher (Q_2).
- *Inward shift in supply:* If the supply curve moves inward (S_1 to S_3), equilibrium moves along DD from E to C. Price is higher (P_3), and quantity demanded/supplied is lower (Q_3).
- In both cases, market equilibrium has changed, but along the *same* demand curve.

Theme 5   ELASTICITY

*E*lasticity is one of the most difficult concepts for the beginning student of economics to grasp. It is a measure of the ratio of the percent change in one variable to the percent change in another. Economists use it to measure how responsive one economic variable is to changes in another. Three significant measures of elasticity usually are introduced in introductory microeconomics courses. Price elasticity of demand describes how quantity demanded reacts to changes in price. Price elasticity of supply describes how quantity supplied changes in response to changes in market price. Income elasticity of demand measures the response of the quantity demanded of a good when consumers' incomes change. Elasticities such as these also can be used to measure how total expenditure upon a good or service can change when its price changes or when incomes of its consumers change.

(**Note:** The *ceteris paribus* assumption (Key 11) applies in all Keys in this Theme.)

INDIVIDUAL KEYS IN THIS THEME

32	Elasticity
33	Arc and midpoint elasticity
34	Price elasticity of demand
35	Elastic and inelastic demand
36	What determines demand elasticity?
37	Price elasticity of supply
38	Elastic and inelastic supply
39	Income elasticity of demand
40	Inferior goods

Key 32   Elasticity

OVERVIEW *Elasticity measures the magnitude of market reactions to changes in price caused by shifts in demand and/or supply. It is expressed as a ratio of the percentage change of one variable relative to the percentage change of another.*

Assumptions (Keys 10–12): *Ceteris paribus*

Elasticity: Elasticity is a measure of the percentage change in one variable (say, X) compared to the percentage change in another (say, Y):

$$E_{xy} = \%\Delta X\ /\ \%\Delta Y$$

- The upper case Greek letter *delta* [Δ] is used by mathematicians to denote "change in."
- According to the laws of algebra, elasticity is positive if the slope of the function it describes is positive. *Example*: A supply curve—when price changes, quantity supplied changes in the *same* direction. Elasticity is negative if the slope is negative. Example: A demand curve—quantity demanded changes in the *opposite* direction from a change in price.
- Price elasticity of demand (Key 34) describes how quantity demanded reacts to changes in price. Price elasticity of supply (Key 37) describes how quantity supplied changes in response to changes in market price. Income elasticity of demand (Key 39) measures the response of the quantity demanded of a good when consumers' incomes change.
- *Important note!* Price elasticity of demand usually comes out negative. Among economists, however, it is conventional to *ignore* its negative sign; we will too. For other elasticity measures, we do not ignore negative status.

Elastic and inelastic demand: If elasticity is greater than 1, then X changes proportionally *more* than Y; such a function is said to be *elastic*. If elasticity is less than 1, then X changes proportionally less than Y; the function is said to be *inelastic*.

Warning! (*For readers who understand differential calculus*): Elasticity is *not* the first derivative of a function! dy/dx measures *absolute* change in x and y at a point. Elasticity measures *percentage* change in x and y at a point or over a range. In a linear function, dy/dx is constant; however, elasticity (being a ratio of *percentage* changes) will be *different* at various points on the *same* linear function.

Key 33   Arc and midpoint elasticities

OVERVIEW *Economists prefer midpoint elasticity to arc elasticity because it yields the same result regardless of the direction of the change.*

Assumptions (Keys 10–12): *Ceteris paribus*

Calculating elasticity: We use *price elasticity of demand* as our example; refer to curve A in the graph in Key 34. *Remember:* This elasticity is shown by economists as a *positive* number (Key 34).

Arc elasticity: Arc elasticity for a *decrease* in P from 14 to 11:

$$\%\Delta P = (14 - 11) / 14 = 0.214 = 21.4\%$$
$$\%\Delta Q_D = (90 - 170) / 90 = -0.889 = 88.9\%$$
$$E_p = \%\Delta Q_D / \%\Delta P = 88.9\% / 21.4\% = \textbf{4.15}$$

Arc elasticity for an *increase* in P from 11 to 14:

$$\%\Delta P = (11 - 14) / 11 = -0.273 = 27.3\%$$
$$\%\Delta Q_D = (170 - 90) / 170 = 0.471 = 47.1\%$$
$$E_p = \%\Delta Q_D / \%\Delta P = 47.1\% / 27.3\% = \textbf{1.724}$$

- A*rc elasticities* differ depending upon the *direction* (up or down) of the price change. This is due to the way we calculate percentages. P decrease from 14 to 11 uses base P of 14 and Q_D of 90. P increase from 11 to 14 uses base P of 11 and Q_D of 170.

Midpoint elasticity: To eliminate this confusion, economists use *midpoint elasticities*. Bases used for P and Q_D are the *midpoints* of the range of change. For the example we used above,

midpoint (P) = $(14 + 11)/2 = 12.5$; midpoint(Q_D) = $(90 + 170)/2 = 130$

When midpoint values are used as the bases, then *over the same range* changes either way in price will result in the *same* value for elasticity.

- For the price *decrease* from 14 to 11,

$$\%\Delta P = (14 - 11) / 12.5 = 0.24 = 24\%$$
$$\%\Delta Q_D = (90 - 170) / 130 = -0.615 = 61.5\%$$
$$E_p = \%\Delta Q_D / \%\Delta P = 61.5\% / 24\% = \textbf{2.564}$$

- For the price *increase* from 11 to 14,

$$\%\Delta P = (11 - 14) / 12.5 = -0.24 = 24\%$$
$$\%\Delta Q_D = (170 - 90) / 130 = 0.615 = 61.5\%$$
$$E_p = \%\Delta Q_D / \%\Delta P = 61.5\% / 24\% = \textbf{2.564}$$

Key 34   Price elasticity of demand

OVERVIEW *Price elasticity of demand is the ratio of the percentage change in quantity demanded to the percentage change in price. When price elasticity of demand is greater than 1, demand is said to be elastic. When price elasticity of demand is less than 1, we say that demand is inelastic. Though this elasticity usually is mathematically negative, economists generally show it as positive.*

Assumptions (Keys 10 –12): *Ceteris paribus*

Measuring price elasticity of demand: *Price elasticity of demand* is measured as the *percentage* change in quantity demanded divided by the *percentage* change in price: $E_p = \%\Delta Q_D\, /\, \%\Delta P$
- We assume prices are set by the market; for clarity, however, market supply curves are not shown in the graph.
- Except for *Giffen goods* (Key 20), price elasticity of demand always is negative because the law of demand states that the demand curve is *negatively* sloped (Key 20). Thus, as price rises (+), quantity demanded falls (–), and vice versa.
- *Important!* Even so, economists usually state price elasticity of demand as a *positive* number.

Elastic and inelastic demand: When price elasticity of demand is less than 1 (Graph A), demand is said to be *inelastic*. When it exceeds 1 (Graph B), demand is *elastic*. (See Key 35 for calculation of elasticities shown in this graph.)

KEY GRAPH

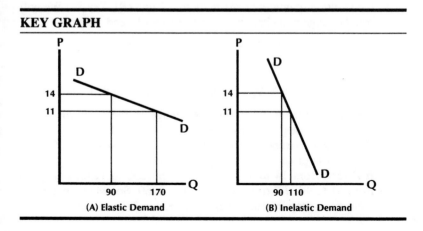

(A) Elastic Demand   (B) Inelastic Demand

Key 35   Elastic and inelastic demand

OVERVIEW *When demand is elastic, percent changes in quantity demanded are greater than percent changes in price. When price falls, total revenue (TR, the total sum spent on the good in the market) increases. When price rises, TR decreases. The reverse is true when demand is inelastic.*

Assumptions (Keys 10–12): *Ceteris paribus*

Effects of elasticity: Price elasticity of demand describes the relationship between changes in price (P) and changes in quantity demanded (Q_D): that is, whether Q_D changes more or less rapidly than does price. It also tells us what happens to *total revenue* (*TR*, the total sum of money spent in the market on the good in question) when price changes and the demand curve *does not shift*. Remember! E_p is shown as a *positive* number (Key 34).

Elastic demand: Graph A in Key 34 shows *elastic* demand, or elasticity *greater* than 1 ($\%\Delta Q_D > \%\Delta P$, so $E_p > 1$).
- Elastic demand: price and *TR* changes are *opposite*. When price rises, *TR* falls; when price falls, *TR* rises.
- *Illustration:* Refer to graph A in Key 34. *TR* at price 14 is (14×90), or 1260. *TR* at price 11 is (11×170), or 1870. So, if price falls from 14 to 11, *TR* rises from 1260 to 1870. If price rises from 11 to 14, *TR* falls from 1870 to 1260.

Inelastic demand: Graph B in Key 34 shows *inelastic* demand, or elasticity *less* than 1 ($\%\Delta Q_D < \%\Delta P$, so $E_p < 1$).
- *Calculation of midpoint elasticity for Graph (B), Key 34:* We will use the range of a change in price between 11 and 14.

$$\%\Delta P = (14 - 11)/12.5 = 0.24 = 24\%$$

$$\%\Delta Q_D = (90 - 110)/100 = \text{-}0.2 = 20\%$$

$$E_p = \%\Delta Q_D \, / \, \%\Delta P = 20\% / \, 24\% = \mathbf{0.833}$$

- Inelastic demand: Price and *TR* change in the *same* direction. When price rises, *TR* rises; when price falls, *TR* falls.
- *Illustration:* (Graph B, Key 34) *TR* at price 14 is (14×90), or 1260. *TR* at price 11 is (11×110), or 1210.
- If *P* falls from 14 to 11, *TR* falls from 1260 to 1210. If *P* rises from 11 to 14, *TR* rises from 1210 to 1260. So, when demand is inelastic, a drop in price results in a drop in *TR* and vice versa.

Key 36   What determines
demand elasticity?

OVERVIEW   *The elasticity of demand is based on four major factors: substitutability, importance, adjustment time, and relative necessity of the good.*

Assumptions (Keys 10–12): *Ceteris paribus*

Determinants of price elasticity of demand: Elasticity of demand reflects the sensitivity of consumers to price changes. Many factors can affect how well and how quickly consumers can adjust to price changes, but economists generally emphasize the four discussed below.

Substitutability: The more close substitutes there are for a good, the more elastic is its demand; the fewer close substitutes, the more inelastic its demand.
- If good X has close substitutes, consumers can switch back and forth between it and its substitutes whenever its price changes. This would imply elastic demand for X.
- If good Y has poor substitutes, consumers aren't able to react to changes in its price by switching to or from substitutes. Therefore their consumption of the good will be less affected by price changes than if they could consider substitutes.

Importance of the good in the consumer's budget: Consumers are not very concerned about prices of goods upon which they spend very little; their demand for them tends to be inelastic. Price changes of goods that they spend a large portion of their budgets on have much more significant effects; demand for such goods tends to be more elastic.

Adjustment time available: The more time consumers have to adjust to price changes of goods, the easier it is for them to find substitutes, rearrange their consumption patterns, etc. Therefore, demand tends to be more elastic the longer the time available to adjust to price changes.

Necessities and luxuries: Demand for goods that consumers consider to be necessities is likely to be more inelastic than demand for luxuries and frills.

Key 37   Price elasticity of supply

OVERVIEW *Price elasticity of supply is the ratio of the percentage change in quantity supplied to the percentage change in price.*

Assumptions (Keys 10–12): *Ceteris paribus*

Measuring price elasticity of supply: *Price elasticity of supply* is measured as the *percentage* change in quantity supplied divided by the *percentage* change in price.

$$E_s = \%\Delta Q_S \, / \, \%\Delta P$$

- When price elasticity of supply is greater than 1, supply is said to be *elastic*; when it is less than 1, then supply is *inelastic*.
- Graph A below shows *elastic* supply; Graph B shows *inelastic* supply. (Prices are set by the market; for purposes of clarity, however, market demand curves are not shown in the graph.)

KEY GRAPH

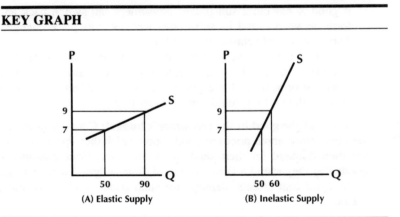

(A) Elastic Supply   (B) Inelastic Supply

Calculating price elasticity of supply: Midpoint supply elasticity is calculated in the same fashion as demand elasticity. Refer to Keys 33 and 35. For price range 7 to 9 in the graph:

- In Graph A midpoint supply elasticity is elastic (more than 1).

$$E_S = \%\Delta Q_S \, / \, \%\Delta P = 57.1\% \, / \, 25\% = \textbf{2.28}$$

- In Graph B midpoint supply elasticity is inelastic (less than 1).

$$E_S = \%\Delta Q_S \, / \, \%\Delta P = 18.2\% \, / \, 25\% = \textbf{0.723}$$

Key 38   Elastic and inelastic supply

OVERVIEW *Price elasticity of supply measures the sensitivity of quantity supplied to changes in demand. When calculated, price elasticity of supply always is positive, so total revenue (TR) always changes the same way that price does.*

Effects of price elasticity of supply: When calculated, price elasticity of supply should be positive. Therefore, when market price changes, total revenue (*TR*) will change in the same direction as price. Increases in price lead to increases in *TR*; decreases in price lead to decreases in *TR*.

Time and elasticity of supply: Elasticity of supply depends partly on the time available for firms to adjust to market price changes.
- In the *long run* all kinds of adjustments can be made, and long-run supply tends to be elastic.
- In the *short run*, firms are restricted by plant capacity, factory, supplies, etc., and cannot easily adjust production. Short-run supply tends to be inelastic.

Perfectly inelastic supply: In some situations, supply cannot change *at all*, no matter how high or low prices go. This is *perfectly inelastic supply,* and the supply curve is graphed as a *vertical* line.
- When supply is perfectly inelastic, shifts in demand change only price and *TR*, since Q_S cannot change.
- The *immediate run* is a time period so short that firms cannot make any adjustments at all; during this time, supply must remain perfectly inelastic.
- For some goods that are very expensive and take a long time to produce (buildings, factories, etc.) the immediate run can be quite a while. Until new ones can be planned, built, and brought on line, the fixed, perfectly inelastic supply of existing ones will be all there is.
- Some goods, by their nature, have a permanently limited supply available, and Q_S can never be augmented. Land and certain rarities (stamps, coins, Van Gogh paintings) are examples. For each there is a fixed amount in existence, and no more can be made.

Key 39   Income elasticity of demand

OVERVIEW *Income elasticity of demand measures the responsiveness of quantity demanded of a good to changes in the incomes of consumers.*

Income elasticity of demand: Quantity demanded of a good responds not just to price but to many other economic influences. An obvious one is consumers' income. Income elasticity of demand measures the sensitivity of quantity demanded of a good to changes in the incomes of consumers who buy it. (*Ceteris paribus* (Key 11) is assumed, especially: all prices remain fixed.) In the formula below, I stands for consumer income.

$$E_I = \%\Delta Q_D \,/\, \%\Delta I$$

For normal goods (Key 40) E_I is positive: Q_D rises or falls as I does.

Income elasticity below 1: Income elasticity is below 1 means that $\Delta Q_D < \%\Delta I$ (the percentage change in Q_D is less than it is for I). This means that income rises or falls faster than Q_D does.
- When $E_I < 1$, then, consumers will spend a smaller fraction of their incomes on the good as their incomes rise, and a larger fraction of their incomes on it when their incomes fall.
- *Example:* Suppose a consumer has a weekly income of $100 and spends $10 of it (10% of income) on milk. E_I for milk is below 1, say 0.9. If income rises by 10%, to $110, E_I tells us that the consumer's Q_D of milk will rise by 9%. Total spent on milk becomes $10.90, falling from 10% to 9.9% of income. If income falls by 10% to $90, milk purchases will fall by 9% to $9.10, which is 10.1% of income.

Income elasticity above 1: When E_I exceeds 1, the reverse is true. As income rises, consumers spend a higher proportion of their income on the good. When income falls, the amount spent on the good becomes a smaller fraction of income.

E_I, luxuries and necessities: Economists say that goods with $E_I > 1$ are luxuries and those with $E_I < 1$ are necessities. When income falls, consumers cut back more on goods they can do without. When income rises, they feel that they can better afford these luxuries, for which E_I, then, exceeds 1.

Key 40   Inferior goods

OVERVIEW *For most goods the income elasticity of demand is positive. Inferior goods are goods for which the income elasticity of demand is negative: that is, as consumer income increases, quantity demanded of inferior goods decreases, and vice versa.*

Assumptions (Keys 10-12): *ceteris paribus*

Normal goods: As mentioned in Key 39, *normal goods* are those for which the income elasticity of demand (E_I) is *positive*. That is, as consumer income rises or falls, the quantity demanded of normal goods rises and falls with income. Most goods are normal goods.

Inferior goods: For a few goods, however, E_I is "wrong"; it is *negative*. These are called *inferior goods*; quantity demanded of them *decreases* as income rises and *increases* as income falls.

Inferior goods and substitutability: The negative E_I for inferior goods usually occurs because there are more desirable, but also *more expensive*, close substitutes for them.
- When their incomes *increase*, consumers are more easily able to buy the preferred, more expensive substitute. When they do, they buy *less* of the inferior good.
- Conversely, when their incomes *fall*, consumers can adjust by substituting the other way. They buy *more* of the inferior good, substituting it for the more expensive normal good.

Inferior good example: Hamburger and sirloin steak are close substitutes. Both are beef, about equally nourishing, etc. But to most consumers steak is tastier and much more desirable. However, it also is much more expensive than hamburger.
- When these consumers' incomes rise, they consume more steak, *substituting* it in their diets for some of the less desirable hamburger they used to buy. Therefore, the increase in income leads them to buy less hamburger.
- When their incomes fall, they cut back their purchases of the more desirable and more expensive steak and substitute the cheaper hamburger for it. The decrease in income has led them to buy *more* hamburger.
- For these consumers, the E_I of hamburger is negative. Hamburger, to them, is an inferior good.

Theme 6   DEMAND: CONSUMER
CHOICE

*C*onsumers allocate their limited incomes so as to buy the goods and services that yield them the most satisfaction (utility). To maximize total utility, they try to arrange their consumption so that the marginal utility per dollar spent on each good is the same; in this manner they spend their incomes most efficiently. Their action is expressed, in the market, as demand. Market demand is the sum of the individual demand curves of all consumers. Because of diminishing marginal utility, consumer demand for normal goods is downward-sloping. Consumers also must consider substitute goods and complementary goods. Indifference curve analysis provides a graphical description of consumer behavior and demand.

INDIVIDUAL KEYS IN THIS THEME

Key 41   Utility and marginal utility

OVERVIEW   *Utility is the satisfaction that consumers receive from consumption of goods and services. Utility is subjective. Individual consumers can measure it for themselves, but economists cannot measure cardinal utility, only ordinal utility. Marginal utility is the additional utility received from the consumption of one more unit of a good or service.*

Definition: Utility is the satisfaction received from the consumption of goods and services. Consumers can measure the utility they get from goods and services and of various combinations (*market baskets*) of them. By doing so, they can determine how to spend their incomes so as to achieve the highest *total utility* (*TU*) from doing so; they *maximize utility* (Key 43).

Cardinal utility: *Cardinal utility* refers to putting an *absolute* measure of utility upon goods and services, or market baskets. Individual consumers can make such judgments: they can say, "I like this twice as much as I like that," etc.
- One cannot make such measures for *other* people, because there is no common *unit of utility* that can be used.
- Because of this, *interpersonal utility comparison* (absolute comparison of one person's level of satisfaction with that of another) cannot be done systematically.

Ordinal utility: *Ordinal utility* measures utility only by *ranking* the consumer's preferences among goods and market baskets. This *can* be measured; one *can* ask consumers if they like A *more* or *less* than B or the *same* as B. This makes possible *rank-ordering* goods and services in order of preference (ordinal utility). "I like this the most, this one next, this one third-best..."*does* mean the same thing from person to person.

Marginal utility: *Marginal utility* (*MU*) of a good or service is the additional utility a consumer receives from consuming one more unit of it *while holding consumption of everything else constant* (*Ceteris paribus,* Key 11). *MU* is a key concept in the theory of consumer behavior that is discussed in this Theme.

Key 42   Diminishing marginal utility

OVERVIEW *For a normal good, marginal utility diminishes as consumption of it is increased.*

Assumptions (Keys 10-12): *CetPar, EcMan*

The law of diminishing marginal utility: This law is a key element in the theory of consumer behavior discussed in this Key. It states that as one consumes more and more of a good or service, its marginal utility declines. That is, as more units are consumed during a particular time period, *total utility* from the good or service increases by less for each additional unit consumed.

Example: Suppose a hungry person enters a restaurant and eats some hamburgers.
- The utility received from the first burger (its *MU*) is quite high; it is very satisfying because the consumer is very hungry.
- If the consumer eats a second one, the utility received from it is *less* than the utility received from the first one. This *MU* of the *second* burger is lower, because the consumer already has had one and isn't so hungry as before.
- By the same reasoning, a third burger may provide some more utility but not as much as the second. *MU* is diminishing with each successive burger.
- This analogy can apply to nearly all goods and services.
- Economists note that for some goods diminishing marginal utility may not be absolutely true, especially for MU at very low levels of consumption. Introductory microeconomics courses usually don't consider these exceptions.

Important! **MU depends upon order in which consumed:** The units of good or service considered in this type of discussion of marginal utility are *identical* (we're always talking about the *same* good or service). In our example, the hamburgers are identical.
- The *MU* of a *particular* unit of that good or service depends upon the *order in which it is consumed* (first one consumed, second one, etc.).
- If our hungry diner had ordered three burgers, we couldn't tell how much *MU* a particular one would provide until the consumer ate them. The *MU* of each *individual* burger depends upon whether it is consumed first, second, etc.

Key 43 Maximizing utility

OVERVIEW *Consumers have limited incomes with which to buy goods and services. Their objective is to maximize utility: to get the most utility possible from spending their incomes.*

Assumptions (Keys 10–12): *CetPar, EcMan, PerfInfo*

Allocating income to maximize utility: Consumers use their incomes to buy goods and services. Their incomes are *limited*, so they can't consume all of everything that they may want. Therefore, consumers act to *allocate* their incomes so as to buy the one combination of goods and services that will give them the highest total utility (*TU*). This is the *principle of utility maximization.*

Utility maximization: Consumers maximize utility by allocating their incomes so that the marginal utility *per dollar spent* is the same for all goods and services consumed.

- The marginal utility of the last unit of good X consumed (MU_X) divided by the price of good X (P_X) must equal the result of the same calculation for good Y, good Z, etc.

$$MU_X/P_X = MU_Y/P_Y = MU_Z/P_Z, \text{ etc.}$$

Example: Assume a consumer starts off in a situation where this is not true. The consumer is choosing among two goods (*pigs* and *figs*), and MU_{pigs}/P_{pigs} is greater than MU_{figs}/P_{figs}.

- The dollars spent to buy the marginal (last one consumed) fig do not produce as much utility as the dollars spent to buy the last pig consumed (the marginal pig).
- Therefore, the consumer could increase his/her total utility by not buying the marginal fig and instead spending the money to buy more pig. Why? Because buying pig with those dollars will yield more utility than spending the same money on fig.
- Once the consumer does this, he/she will be consuming more pig and less fig. Because of diminishing marginal utility, *MU* of pigs will fall (more pig consumed) and *MU* of figs will rise (less fig is consumed).
- Eventually this will result in $MU_{pigs}/P_{pigs} = MU_{figs}/P_{figs}$. Once this becomes the case, there will be no point to any further switching. Total utility will be maximized.

Key 44   Marginal rate of substitution

OVERVIEW   *The marginal rate of substitution (MRS) is the ratio at which consumers are willing to trade between pairs of goods and services at the margin. Along with the price ratio between the goods, it can be used to determine utility maximization.*

Assumptions (Keys 10–12): *CetPar, EcMan, PerfInfo*

Marginal rate of substitution: MU_X / MU_Y is the *marginal rate of substitution* (*MRS*) between good X and good Y. It describes how consumers are willing to trade X for Y, and vice versa.

- If MRS_{XY} is 3, for example, it means that one unit of good X is three times as valuable (has three times the utility) for the consumer as one unit of good Y. The consumer, then, is willing to trade 3 units of Y for 1 unit of X.
- MRS_{XY} will depend upon how much of X and Y the consumer is consuming. For different combinations of the two goods, MRS_{XY} will be different.

Utility maximization using *MRS*: Key 43 describes the condition for utility maximization as $MU_X/P_X = MU_Y/P_Y = MU_Z/P_Z$, etc.

- By algebraic manipulation, the expression above can be rewritten as follows: $MU_X / MU_Y = P_X / P_Y$, etc. From the discussion above, $MU_X / MU_Y = MRS_{XY}$. Therefore, another statement of the condition for utility maximization is $MRS_{XY} = P_X / P_Y$.
- If the price of a unit of X is three times the price of a unit of Y, the price ratio (P_X / P_Y) will be 3. To maximize utility, MRS_{XY} also must be 3, which means that MU_X is 3 times MU_Y.

Example: Suppose $MRS_{XY} = 3$. If $P_X = \$3$, and $P_Y = \$1$, then utility is maximized because $P_X / P_Y = 3/1 = 3 = MRS_{XY}$. If the price of X or Y changes, then P_X / P_Y will not be 3 anymore. The consumer can increase total utility (*TU*) by changing consumption of X and Y.

- Suppose the price of a unit of X rises to \$4; P_X / P_Y will be 4.
- Since MRS_{XY} still is 3, the consumer is willing to trade one of X for three of Y. However, giving up one X now frees up \$4, which will buy four of Y, so the consumer increases TU by consuming one less X and 4 more of Y.
- This will change MRS_{XY}. MU_X will rise (less X is being consumed), and MU_Y will fall (more Y being consumed). MRS_{XY}, then, will increase. The consumer should keep on substituting Y for X until MRS_{XY} rises to the new P_X / P_Y of 4.

Key 45   Income and substitution effects

OVERVIEW *A change in the price of a good influences the household's consumption patterns of all goods. The income effect measures the change in the household's effective income due to the price change. The substitution effect measures the change in consumption of a good because its price has made it relatively cheaper or more expensive.*

Assumptions (Keys 10–12): *CetPar, EcMan, PerfInfo*

Income effect: A change in the price of a good affects the total quantity of goods and services that a household can consume. The *income effect* measures the change in consumption brought on by the change in a consumer's effective income due to a change in price of a good.
- If the price of good *X* falls, the consumer's purchasing power increases. He/she doesn't have to spend as much to achieve the same total utility as before, so there will be income left over to spend on additional consumption. The consumer's same income now will buy *more* total utility than before. His/her *effective income* has risen.
- If the price of *X* rises, the opposite occurs. Now the consumer can no longer afford to buy everything he/she used to; total consumption will have to be cut back. The same income buys less total utility than before; effective income has fallen.

Substitution effect: A change in the price of good X also makes it relatively more attractive (price drop) or less attractive (price increase) in comparison to other goods than it was before the price change. This will lead to a change in consumption of good X as a result of the *substitution effect.* The change in its price makes it more or less attractive relative to other goods.

Example: T-bone steak costs $7 a pound and I buy 3 pounds a week, spending $21 on it. $MU_{t\text{-}bone} / P_{t\text{-}bone} = MU / P$ of other goods: I am maximizing utility (Key 44). T-bone now falls to $5 a pound.
- I now have $6 a week left over to spend on more consumption. I will use some to buy more T-bone steak. The extra T-bone that I buy out of that $6 is a result of the *income effect.*
- However, $MU_{t\text{-}bone} / P_{t\text{-}bone}$ is now higher than MU / P for all other goods. To maximize utility I will buy even more T-bone and less of everything else. This *second* additional quantity of T-bone that I buy is due to the *substitution effect.*

Key 46   Consumer demand,

perceived supply

OVERVIEW *Due to diminishing marginal utility, the consumer's demand for most goods will be downward-sloping. Consumers are price-takers; they perceive the market supply curve, to them, as perfectly elastic.*

Assumptions (Keys 10–12): *CetPar, EcMan, PerfInfo*

Diminishing marginal utility and consumer demand: Key 43 explains that the consumer maximizes utility when the marginal utility per dollar spent on each good consumed is the same:

$$MU_X/P_X = MU_Y/P_Y = MU_Z/P_Z, \text{ etc.}$$

- If the consumer consumes any more of a good, its *MU* will fall because of the law of diminishing marginal utility.
- So, if the consumer consumes more of good X, MU_X will fall. If the consumer is to continue maximizing utility, then in order for the equality $MU_X/P_X = MU_Y/P_Y = MU_Z/P_Z$, etc., to hold, P_X (the price of X) also must fall.
- Therefore, the utility-maximizing consumer will buy more of a good only if its price falls; the consumer's demand curve for the good, therefore, slopes *downward*.

The consumer's perception of supply: Consumers usually are thought of by economists as *price-takers*.

- This means that, since each consumer is only one of a great many, none of them has enough influence in the market to affect market price with his/her activity alone.
- Therefore, consumers expect the market price for each good or service to remain unchanged no matter how much or how little the individual consumer chooses to buy. To the consumer, therefore, market supply is perceived as *perfectly elastic*. (See the graph in Key 48.)

Market demand: Market demand for a good or service is the *sum* of all individual consumers' demand. At each price, each consumer is willing to buy a certain amount. The total of these amounts will be the quantity demanded in the market at that price—the total quantity demanded at that price by all consumers together.

Key 47   Substitute and complementary goods

OVERVIEW *Substitute goods are goods that are easily exchangeable for one another in consumption. When the price of one falls, consumption of the other falls, and vice versa. Complementary goods are those that must be consumed together.*

Assumptions (Keys 10-12): *CetPar, EcMan, PerfInfo*

Substitute goods: Substitute goods are those that the consumer can exchange for one another in his/her consumption patterns. The consumer cannot distinguish between *perfect substitutes* at all. He/she consumes only the cheapest, and none of the others.

- The consumer can tell the difference between *close substitutes* and may consume some of each, but he/she is still very sensitive to their substitutability. A change in price of one will lead to changes in the consumption of all of them.
- If the price of one close substitute rises, the consumer will buy less of it and more of the other. If its price falls, the reverse will happen.
- *Example of perfect substitutes:* Some people can't tell, or don't care about, the difference between Coke and Pepsi. To them, these are perfect substitutes; they consume only the cheapest.
- *Example of close substitutes:* Some people find a difference between the two drinks and also prefer one to the other. They buy the one they like, unless the other costs less. Then they will consider substituting some of the other cheaper one for their preferred drink.

Complementary goods: Complementary goods are goods that consumers like to consume *together*. (This also is sometimes referred to as *joint consumption*.)

- *Examples of complementary goods*: automobiles, tires, and gasoline; compact discs and CD players; VCRs and videotape; bacon and eggs, etc.
- If the price of a complementary good rises, consumption of it *and its complement* will fall, and vice versa.
- Their complementary use leads the consumer to consider the complementary combination of goods, to some extent, to be a *single* good.

Key 48 Consumer surplus

OVERVIEW *Consumers pay the same price for all units of a good. However, they actually receive more total utility than is "paid for." This extra utility is consumer surplus.*

Assumptions (Keys 10–12): *CetPar, EcMan, PerfInfo*

Graph: The graph shows the consumer's demand curve (D) for a good and the consumer's perfectly elastic perception of market supply (Key 46) at price P_M; the consumer will buy quantity Q_D.

Consumer surplus: If the consumer is maximizing utility, then P_M is a money measure of what the last unit consumed of the good (the marginal unit) is worth to the consumer.

KEY GRAPH

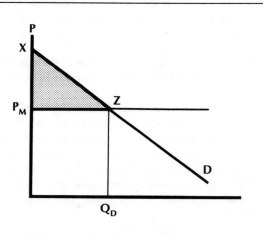

- However, because of diminishing marginal utility, *MU* of the *other* units consumed *exceeds MU* of the marginal unit. Demand curve D shows that the consumer would have been willing to pay *more* than P_M for each of those units, because of their higher *MU*. Still, they cost only P_M apiece.
- For these other units, the consumer receives more *MU* per dollar spent than for the marginal unit. This extra total utility is called *consumer surplus*. In the graph, consumer surplus is the shaded area $X – P_M$-Z.

Key 49 Indifference curves

OVERVIEW *Indifference curves are graphical represen-tations used in some microeconomics courses to help demonstrate consumer behavior and choice.*

Assumptions (Keys 10-12): *CetPar, EcMan, PerfInfo*

Indifference curves: *Indifference curves* are shown on the consumer's *indifference map*, which is a diagram like the one below. The graph shows a two-good model.
- Each of the curved lines is made up of combinations of good *A* and good *B* that all yield the *same* utility.
- Since all the combinations on one line are of equal utility to the consumer, he/she is *indifferent* to which is actually consumed. That is why they are called *indifference curves*.

KEY GRAPH

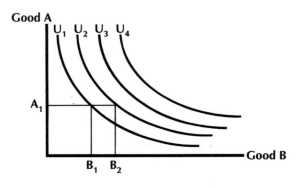

Indifference curves and total utility: Each indifference curve shows a *different* level of total utility. The higher (further out) they are, the more *TU* they represent. In the diagram, curve U_4 represents more total utility than U_3, which is more than U_2, etc.
- This can also be shown by examining combinations on two dif-ferent curves which include the *same* amount of one good.

- For example, one combination on curve U_1 is quantity A_1 of good A and B_1 of good B. Moving to curve U_2, the consumer can consume the same amount of A while increasing consumption of B to B_2. Clearly, then, indifference curve U_2 must represent greater total utility, since it can allow consumption of more of B without requiring any A to be given up.

Key 50   Utility maximization (graph)

OVERVIEW *The consumer's indifference map can be used to demonstrate utility maximization.*

Assumptions (Keys 10–12): *CetPar, EcMan, PerfInfo*

KEY GRAPH

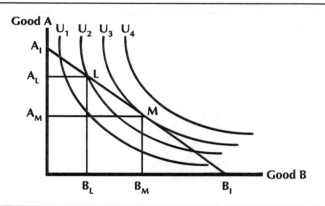

Budget restraint: The *budget restraint* (line A_IB_I) on the indifference map shows all the combinations of good A and good B that the consumer's limited income will allow him/her to buy.
- The location of the budget restraint depends upon the prices of A and B. If no B is bought, the consumer can buy quantity A_I of good A. If no A is bought, the consumer can buy quantity B_I of good B. Other points on the budget restraint are the other affordable combinations of A and B. For example, if A_L of A is bought, there will be income left over to buy B_L of B as well.

Utility maximization: The consumer maximizes utility by buying the one combination of goods on the budget restraint that is *tangent* to (just grazes) the *highest* indifference curve. This provides the most total utility obtainable with the consumer's limited income. In the diagram, the highest achievable indifference curve is U_3. The income restraint is *tangent* to U_3 at point M. To maximize utility, the consumer should buy A_M of A and B_M of B. Any other *affordable* combination (say, L) will be on a *lower* indifference curve, and the consumer will become better off by choosing combination M instead.

OVERVIEW *This Key describes the income and substitution effects using the indifference map.*

Assumptions (Keys 10–12): *CetPar, EcMan, PerfInfo*

KEY GRAPH

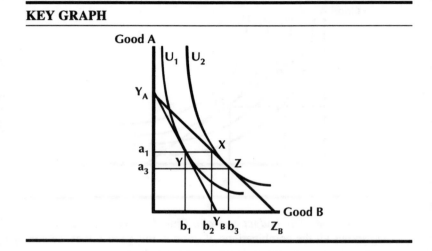

Income and substitution effects: The consumer starts out with budget restraint $Y_A Y_B$. To maximize utility (Key 50) combination Y of the two goods is chosen: a_1 of A, and b_1 of B. The consumer is on the highest indifference curve attainable: U_1. Now the price of B falls, and the budget restraint moves to $Y_A Z_B$. This is because for each possible quantity of A purchased, the money left over to buy B will buy more B at the lower price.

Income effect: At combination X, on the new budget restraint the consumer increases purchases of B from b_1 to b_2 without changing consumption of A. This additional consumption of B (the quantity $b_1 b_2$) results from the *income effect* of the fall in price of B. The drop in price of B leaves the consumer with income left over when the original combination Y is bought; the consumer's *effective* income has increased.

Substitution effect: Although combination X represents more total utility than combination Y, the consumer still has not maximized utility from the drop in price in B. The income restraint reaches the highest indifference curve possible (U_2) at combination Z. Combination X is below U_2, so the consumer can raise total utility even more by changing consumption to combination Z.

- To move from combination X to combination Z, the consumer buys an additional quantity b_2b_3 of B, reducing consumption of A from a_1 to a_3. This is the *substitution effect*. The additional quantity b_2b_3 of B is *substituted* in place of the quantity a_1a_3 of A which is given up. Utility is now maximized.

Key 52 Downward-sloping demand (graph)

OVERVIEW *Downward-sloping demand can be demonstrated using the indifference map.*

Assumptions (Keys 10-12): *CetPar, EcMan, PerfInfo*

Indifference map and downward-sloping demand: The top graph is an indifference map showing quantities of *A* and *B* consumed at three different prices for B: $7, $5, and $3.
  • The price of A, which we will say is everything else, does not change.
  • The three separate budget restraints reflect the different prices of *B*.
  • For the different prices of *B*, the top graph shows that the consumer will buy quantity b_7 of B at $7, quantity b_5 at $5, and quantity b_3 at $3.

The consumer's demand curve for good *B*: The lower graph shows the consumer's demand curve (line *D*) for *B* resulting from graphing the quantities b_7, b_5, and b_3 with the prices of $7, $5, and $3.
  • The horizontal axes on both graphs are the same: they show, on the same scale, the quantity demanded of *B*.
  • The resulting demand curve *D* slopes downward: larger quantities of *B* will be consumed as P_B falls (the law of demand).

KEY GRAPH

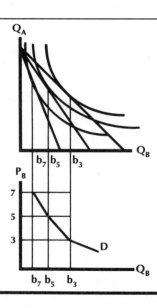

66

Key 53 Social indifference curves

OVERVIEW *Social indifference curves are for the entire society as a whole. The social indifference map can be used with the PPF to determine the allocatively efficient combination of goods for the society as a whole.*

Assumptions (Keys 10–12): *CetPar, EcMan, PerfInfo*

KEY GRAPH

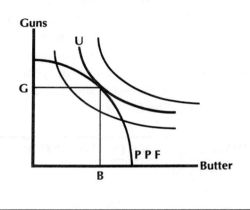

Social indifference map: The *social indifference map* looks just like the consumer's indifference map. The difference is that it shows the same thing *for the society as a whole*.

The PPF as society's "budget restraint": The society is "restrained" by its scarce resources (Key 2). The possible combinations of goods that can be produced with these scarce resources are shown by the PPF.
- The PPF shows all the *technically* efficient combinations of guns and butter that can be produced with the society's resources.
- In the graph, the darker social indifference curve is the highest one that the PPF is tangent to. This means that quantity *G* of guns and quantity *B* of butter is the *allocatively* efficient combination for the society.

Theme 7 THE FIRM: COSTS

*T*he firm's costs are the total of the payments that the firm has to make for everything that has to do with its operations. These include labor, equipment, raw materials, and everything else that it has to spend to run its business and to stay in business. Economists recognize two types of costs: fixed costs and variable costs. Together, these add up to total costs. The law of diminishing returns states that the productivity of an input falls as the amount used of it increases with respect to other inputs. Average total costs and average variable costs reflect the changes in costs per unit of production as production level changes. Marginal cost is a measure of the cost of an additional unit of production and is used in Themes 8 and 9 to determine the equilibrium levels of production for the firm.

Key 54   Fixed cost

OVERVIEW *Fixed costs are those costs of production that remain the same no matter how much—or how little—output the firm produces.*

Assumptions (Keys 10–12): *Ceteris paribus*

Fixed costs: These costs exist and do not change no matter how much or how little the firm produces.
- *Important:* Fixed costs *are not* affected by the firm's level of production. Any cost that changes as the level of production changes is *not* a fixed cost. It is a *variable cost* (Key 55).
- Total fixed cost (*FC*) is the sum of all of the firm's separate fixed costs. A graph shows *FC* as a horizontal line, since at all levels of production (*Q*), fixed costs remain the same.
- The only way the firm can avoid paying fixed costs is to go out of business altogether.

KEY GRAPH

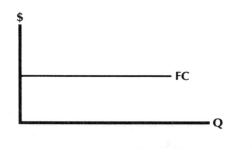

Examples of fixed costs: Since fixed costs are independent of the level of production, they can include only those costs that do not change as production changes. *Examples:*
- *rent payments* for facilities, equipment
- *debt payments* on loans, mortgages
- *salaries* of permanent personnel who remain employed regardless of production level (e.g., managers)
- *insurance premiums, license fees*
- certain taxes, such as *property taxes* and *privilege taxes*; (but not income taxes, sales taxes, and excise taxes because those vary as production varies and so are variable costs).

Key 55 Variable cost

OVERVIEW *Variable costs rise and fall as the firm's output level rises and falls.*

Assumptions (Keys 10–12): *Ceteris paribus, PerfInfo*

Variable costs: Variable costs are those costs that change as the firm's quantity of output changes.
- The most common examples of variable costs are payments for *labor* and *raw materials*. Some other examples of variable costs are utilities, overtime pay, advertising, and waste disposal.
- As production increases, more labor must be hired to make it, and more raw materials must be purchased to make it with.
- The firm's variable cost (*VC*) is the total of all the separate variable costs incurred.

KEY GRAPH

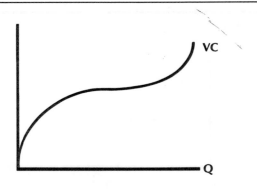

Behavior of variable cost: As output increases, *VC* increase at different rates. As output (*Q*) increases, we expect *VC* to rise rapidly at first, then level off, and finally begin to increase rapidly again.
- At low levels of production, many resources are not being fully used. Equipment has to be bought or rented, people hired, etc. even though the production level is not great enough to employ them in the most efficient combinations.
- When production is high, diminishing returns (Key 56) cause variable costs to accelerate.
- Between these extremes, most resources are used efficiently, and variable costs rise more slowly.

Key 56   Diminishing returns

OVERVIEW *As the use of a variable input is increased in a production process, with all other inputs remaining fixed, its productivity eventually will decline. This is the law of diminishing returns.*

Assumptions (Keys 10–12): *Ceteris paribus, PerfInfo*

Diminishing returns: If the use of a variable input (a resource used in the firm's production process) increases while the other inputs being used remain fixed, at some point the productivity of the variable input will decline. This is the *law of diminishing returns.*

- Another way of stating the law of diminishing returns is to consider that as an economy puts its resources into use, the most productive will be used first. As the economy's output increases, its less productive resources will be put into use. Consequently, as production increases, the *marginal physical product* (Key 90) of inputs decreases.

Diminishing returns and variable costs: Variable costs (Key 55) are the costs of variable inputs; fixed costs (Key 54) are the costs of fixed inputs. When we consider variable and fixed inputs together, we see that diminishing returns can eventually affect the variable inputs.

- Fixed inputs (plant, major equipment, etc.) don't change. Variable inputs (labor, materials, etc.) can be increased and decreased. When variable inputs are changed within a given base of fixed inputs, output will change.
- When output reaches a high enough level, inefficiency will become a problem. Diminishing returns will set in.
- This can happen for many reasons. Production lines (a fixed input) will become crowded and overused by the variable inputs; they will work less efficiently when they are bumping into one another, getting in each other's way, etc. Bottlenecks can develop; once a part of the production process begins to become crowded or overextended, its inefficiency can affect the rest of the production process.
- Since variable inputs become less efficient when diminishing returns sets in, the amount of variable inputs needed to add a given amount to output will increase. This means that the cost of the variable inputs (variable costs) also will increase, as described by the graph in Key 55.

Key 57 Short-run and long-run costs

OVERVIEW *In the short run, costs tend to be fixed. In the long run, they tend to be variable.*

Assumptions (Keys 10–12): *Ceteris paribus, PerfInfo*

Short-run and long-run variable costs: Depending upon the time element involved, certain costs can be either variable or fixed. The theory of the firm usually considers the *short run* and the *long run*.

- The short run is defined as a period of time so short that at least one factor of production is fixed. (The *immediate run* is a period so short that *all* costs are fixed.)
- The *long run* is defined as that period of time long enough that *all costs are variable.*

The importance of time in making changes: Making changes takes time. The more significant the changes, the more time they usually take. In the short run, firms can change such things as employment of some labor, quantities of some other resources used, etc. It takes more time (long run) to change significant aspects of the production process, such as introducing new technology, changing plant size or layout or significantly changing the way inputs are used, the combinations in which they are used, or even the kinds of inputs themselves.

- In the short run, many parameters of the firm's production process cannot be changed and so the costs associated with them are considered fixed. *Examples:* costs of plant, equipment, and core management.
- Over longer periods of time many of these things *can* be changed, and these *short-run fixed costs* become *long-run variable costs.* Given enough time, almost anything about a production process can be changed: new plants can be built, new heavy equipment installed, management (indeed, even the entire firm) reorganized, etc. To economists, the long run is the period of time so long that *all* costs become variable.
- The analysis of the firm in microeconomics tends to consider the short run. The long run is described in greater detail in Key 62.

Key 58 Total cost

OVERVIEW *Total cost is the sum of fixed cost and variable cost. Since total fixed costs are unchanging, total costs vary with total variable costs.*

Assumptions (Keys 10–12): *CetPar, PerfInfo*

Total costs: Total cost (*TC*) is the sum of fixed cost and variable cost: $FC + VC = TC$. In the diagram, output is shown horizontally and costs vertically.
- Fixed cost is shown as a straight line (Key 54) because it never changes, regardless of the amount of output.
- Variable cost (Key 55) increases as output increases.
- In the graph, *VC* is shown *above FC*, since the two are added together to determine *TC*.

KEY GRAPH

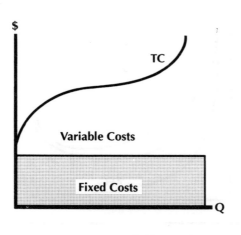

- As described in Key 55, *VC* increases rapidly at first, then more slowly (diminishing returns, Key 56) as output grows. Finally, when output becomes very large, *VC* increases rapidly again.
- Total cost performs the same way: when $Q = 0$, then $TC = FC$. *TC* then rises rapidly at first, then more slowly. When *Q* becomes very high, *TC* rises more rapidly.

Key 59   AVC, AFC, and ATC

OVERVIEW   *Average variable cost, AVC, is the mean value of variable cost (or variable cost per unit of output) at each level of output. Average fixed cost, AFC, is the mean value of fixed cost. Average total cost, ATC, is the mean value of total cost (or cost per unit of output) at each level of output. They are used in the determination of the firm's equilibrium level of production.*

Assumptions (Keys 10–12): *CetPar, PerfInfo*

Definitions: *Average variable cost* (*AVC*) is variable cost divided by output. *Average fixed cost* (*AFC*) is fixed cost divided by output. *Average total cost* (*ATC*) is total cost divided by output.

$$AVC = VC/Q; \quad AFC = FC/Q; \quad ATC = TC/Q$$

KEY GRAPH

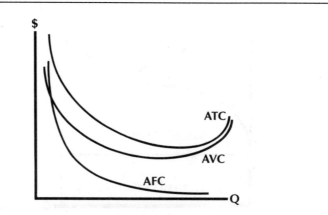

Behavior of *ATC*, *AVC*, and *AFC*: Both *ATC* and *AVC* are high at low levels of output. They decline as output increases. As output increases further, both eventually begin to rise again.

- As output (*Q*) increases, fixed cost (*FC*) does not change. Therefore, as *Q* increases, *AFC*, which is *FC/Q*, must decrease.
- *TC* = *VC* + *FC* (Key 58). Therefore, *ATC* = *AVC* + *AFC*. Since *AFC* is the difference between *ATC* and *AVC*, this means that as output increases, *AVC* and *ATC* get closer together, because *AFC* is getting smaller and smaller.

Key 60   Marginal cost

OVERVIEW *Marginal cost (MC) is the cost that the firm must incur to increase output by one more unit.*

Assumptions (Keys 10–12): *CetPar, PerfInfo*

Definition: Marginal cost (*MC*) is the increase in total cost incurred to produce an additional unit of output. The *MC* of producing *any* unit of output is only the *additional* variable cost that will be incurred for the production of *that one unit.*

KEY GRAPH

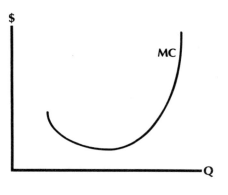

Example: A firm increases output from 19 units to 20.
- *MC* of the 20th unit produced is the total cost of producing all 20 units, *less* the total cost of producing the first 19 units.
- Therefore, *MC* of the *20th* unit is the *additional cost* incurred to increase production *from 19 units to 20 units.*

$$MC_{20th\ unit} = TC_{20\ units} - TC_{19\ units}$$

- Since *FC* is the same at all production levels, the only change in cost to produce additional units is a change in *variable* costs (Key 55). Therefore, we also can say that *MC* is the additional variable cost incurred to produce the additional unit of output.

$$MC_{20th\ unit} = VC_{20\ units} - VC_{19\ units}$$

Behavior of marginal cost: At very low levels of production, *MC* falls rapidly. Then, depending upon the behavior of the firm's variable costs, it decreases more slowly. As output continues to increase, diminishing returns (Key 56) set in. *VC* begins to rise more rapidly. Therefore, *MC* begins to rise and continues to do so as output increases further. (Key 90 describes the behavior of MC with respect to marginal physical product.)

Key 61 MC, ATC, and AVC

OVERVIEW *The MC curve intersects AVC and ATC curves, from below, at their lowest points.*

Assumptions (Keys 10–12): *CetPar, PerfInfo*

Relationship between *MC*, *ATC*, and *AVC*: So long as *MC* remains below *AVC* (Key 59), *AVC* will decline as output increases.
- The cost of each successive unit (which is *MC*) is *less* than *AVC* to that point and therefore reduces the average when it is added into the calculation.
- Once *MC* begins to increase, it eventually will reach the point at which *MC* = *AVC*. Beyond this point, *MC* > *AVC* (*MC* is greater than *AVC*). Therefore, *AVC* will begin to *increase* as output expands.
- The same logic also shows that as long as *MC* is below *AC*, *AC* will fall; once *MC* exceeds *ATC*, *AC* will begin to rise.

KEY GRAPH

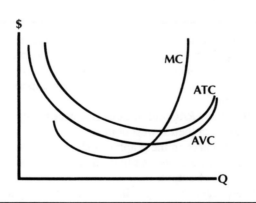

***MC* intersects *ATC* and *AVC* at their lowest points:** The discussion above tells us that the *rising MC* curve *always* intersects the *AVC* curve at its *lowest* point.
- The same logic shows that the rising *MC* curve also intersects *ATC* at the lowest point on the *ATC* curve.
- This relationship between *MC*, *AVC*, and *ATC* is essential to determination of the firm's equilibrium (how much it will produce and what price it will get for its product in the market).

Key 62   The long-run AC curve

OVERVIEW *In the long run, all costs become variable. The long-run average cost curve is generated by "enveloping" along a succession of short-run AC curves.*

Assumptions (Keys 10–12): *CetPar, PerfInfo*

KEY GRAPH

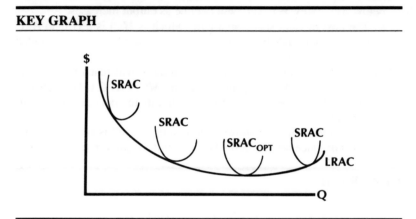

Long-run average cost curve (*LRAC*): In the long run (a matter of as much as decades in some industries), *all* costs become variable (Key 57). The long-run average cost curve, *LRAC*, "envelopes" the short run average cost curves (*SRAC*) that the firm experiences at various levels of output.
  * Note that the *LRAC* curve does not necessarily "envelope" the *SRAC* curves at their lowest points.
  * Each *SRAC* curve in the graph is a short-run *ATC* curve (Key 59) with the firm using the optimum amount of plant and equipment for that level of output.
  * The *LRAC* curve usually falls over a considerable portion of its length due to *economies of scale* (Key 63). At very high output levels, the *LRAC* curve may rise due to *diseconomies of scale* (Key 63).

Optimum plant size: Optimum plant size, operated at the optimum rate of output, occurs at the lowest point on the *LRAC* curve. This is the *single* point on *LRAC* where *LRAC* is tangent to the lowest point on a *SRAC* curve (the one marked *SRAC_OPT*). At all other points on *LRAC*, the tangency with *SRAC* curves occurs somewhere other than the lowest points on these other *SRAC* curves.

Key 63   Economies and
diseconomies of scale

OVERVIEW *An industry has economies of scale if larger plant and firm sizes increase efficiency, and therefore incur lower average costs as size becomes larger. Economies of scale exist when the LRAC curve declines as production increases. Diseconomies of scale occur when the LRAC curve rises.*

Definition: *Economies of scale* (also called *increasing returns to scale*) exist when larger plant or firm sizes are more efficient (produce at lower cost) than smaller sizes. Note that although a portion of the short-run *ATC* curve (Key 59) does decline, economies of scale refer only to the long run average cost curve (*LRAC*, Key 62). This is because increasing firm size in order to lower average costs can't be done in the short run.

Causes: Many factors can create economies of scale:
- Some production processes are efficient only if large quantities are produced (assembly lines, automation).
- Large scale can allow use of more specialized (i.e.: more efficient) factors of production (labor, equipment, etc.)
- Firms with high capital costs (equipment, etc.) can spread such costs over larger outputs and thus experience falling long run average costs over considerable ranges of production.

Behavior of economies of scale: Economies of scale behave differently in different industries.
- Some heavy industries (autos, steel, etc.) show economies of scale up to very great size. This is because they use large plants and have heavy investment in fixed equipment. They also benefit from use of specialized inputs.
- In some industries there may not be enough demand to warrant large plant or firm sizes. In others, such as those where personal service to customers is significant, large size may not increase efficiency.

Diseconomies of scale: In almost any industry, it is possible for firms to be *too* big. Thus, economies of scale exist only up to a point. Beyond it, *diseconomies of scale* occur. These usually are caused by difficulties in management and organization, such as bureaucracy or difficulties with information—managing it, processing it, conveying it.

Theme 8   PROFIT MAXIMIZATION AND PERFECT COMPETITION

*I*n any markets, firms try to maximize profits by seeking to produce at the point where total revenue exceeds total cost by the largest margin. This equilibrium point occurs where marginal revenue and marginal cost are equal. In perfectly competitive markets, the equilibrium point for firms in the market has one more condition—that marginal revenue, marginal cost, and average costs are equal.

INDIVIDUAL KEYS IN THIS THEME

Key 64   Competition

OVERVIEW *Competition exists in any market in which more than a single firm operates. Competition requires firms to consider and be affected by the actions of the other firms in the industry.*

Competition: Competition for scarce resources exists in every economy. Indeed, if there were no scarce resources, there wouldn't be much point to the study of economics.

Property rights: In all but the most centrally-controlled economies, there are private property rights to scarce resources. These rights are recognized, enforced, and defended by society's legal system.
- Without such rights, the acquisition and allocation of resources would be a chaotic battle between the weak and the strong.
- People own the property rights to their own labor. Some people and firms own the property rights to the other nonlabor resources in the economy.

Need for competition: In order for property rights to have real meaning, they must be freely exchangeable. This usually is accomplished in competitive markets where those who want to use the resources may bid for them. Thus, the resources will be used by those who will pay the most for them, presumably because they anticipate greater profit from their use than anyone else.

Market models: In the theory of the firm, economists recognize four different market models with varying degrees of competitiveness: *Perfect competition* (Keys 68–72): many buyers, many small firms, homogeneous product (Key 66), free entry and exit (Key 67); *monopolistic competition* (Keys 79–80): same conditions as perfect competition, except that there is product differentiation (Key 66); *oligopoly* (Keys 81–84): a few large firms with or without other small firms, product differentiation (Key 66), some barriers to entry and exit (Key 67), and *monopoly* (Keys 75–78): one single firm dominates the market, very difficult entry (Key 67) by other firms.

Key 65 Efficiency

OVERVIEW *Economists recognize several types of efficiency of production: technical efficiency, economic efficiency, and allocative efficiency.*

Assumptions (Keys 10–12): *Ceteris paribus*

Technical efficiency: Technical efficiency exists within the firm whenever using a lower quantity of any input will require using more of at least one other input in order to maintain the same level of output. Technical efficiency refers to the different ways in which a firm can combine inputs in order to produce a certain quantity of output.

Economic efficiency: Economic efficiency exists when the firm, at a given level of output, is using the one technically efficient combination of resources that results in the lowest cost to the firm of producing *that amount of output.*

Allocative efficiency: Allocative efficiency refers to the one *level of output* at which the firm's average cost (*ATC*, Key 59) is lowest. The firm is able to be economically efficient at many levels of output; however, the *ATC* will vary among them. The allocatively efficient one is the one at which ATC is lowest. The result is that if the firm's production is allocatively efficient, it is producing output at the lowest possible cost.

Note!: All of these depend upon many factors: input prices (Theme 10), market price of the output, the production function (Key 89). If any of these change, then the points at which any of these kinds of efficiency occur may change as well.

Key 66   Homogeneous and
differentiated product

OVERVIEW *Homogeneous product exits in an industry when no firm's product can be distinguished from other firms'. Product differentiation occurs when some distinction exists among products produced by each of the firms.*

Assumptions (Keys 10–12): *Ceteris paribus*

Product homogeneity: When firms within an industry produce identical products, their product is said to be *homogeneous* (which means "the same"). *Product homogeneity* exists in such industries.
- It is a characteristic of perfect competition (Keys 68–69).
- To a buyer, the only possible reason for preferring one firm's output to another's is lower price.
- *Example:* Many farm products are homogeneous. If a grain elevator is full of soybeans, you can't tell one farmer's beans from another, and you don't care.

Product differentiation: *Differentiated* product exists when you can tell a difference (or think you can) between different firms' products within the same industry. *Product differentiation is nonprice competition.* By making their products actually or seemingly somewhat different, firms try to create customer loyalty (preference among consumers for their product).
- Product differentiation is a feature of *monopolistic competition* (Keys 79–80) and, sometimes, *oligopoly* (Keys 81–85).
- Strong customer loyalty makes the demand for the firm's product less elastic. The firm loses fewer customers when new firms enter the market and is less vulnerable to their competition.
- The firm attempts, through nonprice competition, to shift the demand curve for its product to the right. It attracts customers by improving the firm's product or service.
- Nonprice competition that cannot be duplicated by other competing firms, such as establishing a *brand name* favored by consumers, is especially effective. *Advertising* can create differentiation and customer loyalty, especially when establishing and maintaining brand-name identification of the firm's product.

Key 67   Ease of entry and exit

OVERVIEW *Barriers to entry to an industry or market, such as high startup costs, are important features of less competitive markets such as monopolistic competition and oligopoly.*

Assumptions (Keys 10–12): *Ceteris paribus*

Industry entry and exit: A significant aspect of any industry, and the competitiveness within it, is the degree to which firms can enter or leave it. When entry and exit is easy, the industry is likely to be very competitive. Less competitive markets have barriers of some kind, especially to entry by new firms. Ease of entry is, in economics, much more significant, since it affects the ability of new competition to arise within an industry or market. Exit from most markets is relatively easy, anyway; there is little to prevent a firm from closing down.
- Entry into a market is easy when there are few or no effective barriers to new firms wishing to enter. Ease of entry is a condition for perfect competition (Keys 68–72).
- A market with difficult entry has barriers of some kinds to new firms. The barriers, to some degree, insulate firms in the market from new competitors and tend to make the market less competitive. Easy entry exists in monopolistic competition (Keys 79–80). Strong barriers are a feature of oligopoly (Keys 81–84). Insurmountable barriers (impossible entry) exist in monopolistic markets (Keys 75–78).

Economic barriers: *High startup costs* are one of the most effective barriers to new firms entering an industry. Newcomers simply can't afford it. While there is no law against starting a new automobile company, the immense cost of design, engineering, factories, sales outlets, etc., keeps new competitors out. Large *economies of scale* (Key 63) are an effective barrier, since they lead to high startup costs.

Noneconomic barriers: *Government franchise* grants a firm exclusive rights to operate within a certain area and effectively keeps all other firms out. *Private franchise* protects a firm against local competition from the same brand-name franchisor but cannot protect against other firms selling similar products of another brand. *Licensing, zoning,* and other government action can keep out competition.

Key 68   Perfect competition

OVERVIEW *Perfect competition is characterized by many buyers, many small firms, a homogeneous product, and free entry and exit.*

Assumptions (Keys 10–12): *CetPar, EffMar, PerfInfo, Costless, Instant*

Characteristics of perfect competition: In economic theory, perfectly competitive markets have certain characteristics:

- *Many small firms*: Perfectly competitive markets contain a great many small firms. No single firm is so large that its own individual actions can have any perceptible effect upon the market as a whole.
- *Homogeneous output:* All firms in the market produce exactly the same product. There is no product differentiation. No buyer can distinguish the product of one of the firms from that of any other (Key 66).
- *No barriers to entry and exit*: Firms can enter and leave the industry freely, instantly, and costlessly (Key 67).
- *Perfect information:* Buyers and sellers have perfect information (Key 12) about market prices and product.
- *Firms are price takers*: Each firm has to accept the market price as a given quantity, outside its control or influence (more about this in Key 69).

Warning! The economic theory of perfect competition is probably the most intellectually satisfying theory in any of the social sciences. It works out beautifully, logically, and indisputably, without any loose ends. As a result, many people seem to rely upon it as a basis for belief that unfettered, free markets inevitably lead to economic efficiency. There are several problems here: First, the assumptions and conditions behind the theory of perfect competition may not always be realistic. Second, a major thrust of the economic theory behind the other market models (monopoly, monopolistic competition, and oligopoly) is that they are *not* economically efficient. Finally, many economists contend that in the real world there really isn't much perfect competition at all: most markets actually are variants of the other three. This is not the place to debate such an issue. The warning here is that you should not make up your mind about economic systems until you have studied and understood a lot more of economic theory than just this one model.

Key 69   Total revenue and
marginal revenue

OVERVIEW *In perfect competition, the firm's marginal revenue (MR) is the market price, and the firm perceives a perfectly elastic market demand curve for its product: D = MR = P.*

Assumptions (Keys 10–12): *CetPar, EffMar, PerfInfo, Costless, Instant*

Total revenue: The firm's *total revenue (TR)* is the total sum for which it is able to sell the total quantity of product that it supplies.

KEY GRAPH

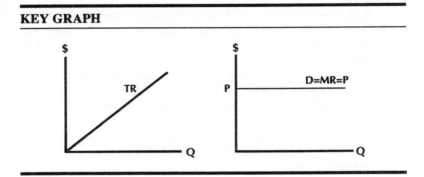

Marginal revenue: A firm's *marginal revenue (MR)* is the increase in total revenue brought about by an increase of one unit of output in the firm's quantity supplied.

***TR, MR,* and perceived demand in perfect competition:** The perfectly competitve firm is called a *price taker* because it receives the *same* market price (*P*) for *every* unit of its output. The perfectly competitive firm is so small that it cannot influence market price in any way, and it accepts the market price as a given condition.

- The firm's *TR* always rises by the market price *P* for each additional unit produced. A graph of the perfectly competitive firm's TR curve is a continually rising straight line.
- The firm's marginal revenue is always the market price: *MR = P*.
- The firm will view market demand for its output as *perfectly elastic*. It can sell all it can for price *P*. *P* is also the same as *MR*, so for the perfectly competitive firm, *D = MR = P*.

Key 70   Profit maximization

OVERVIEW *The firm achieves profit maximization (equilibrium) when marginal revenue equals marginal cost. At any other point, profit will be lower.*

Assumptions (Keys 10–12): *CetPar, EffMar, PerfInfo, Costless, Instant*

Profit maximization: The firm's economic objective is to *maximize profits*. To do this, it seeks to operate so that the difference between its total revenue (Key 69) and total cost (Key 58) is the largest possible; this difference is the firm's *profit: $\pi = TR - TC$*. (Economists use the Greek letter π, or *pi*, to denote profit.)

- *Important note:* The term *profit*, as economists discuss it in the theory of the firm, refers only to profit that exceeds *normal profit*. As explained in Key 16, normal profit is a *cost*.

The profit maximization rule $MR = MC$: Profit maximization occurs at that Q of output where the marginal cost (MC) curve (Key 60) intersects the marginal revenue (MR) curve (Key 69) from below. This is a universal rule. It applies whether or not the firm is a perfect competitor.

KEY GRAPH

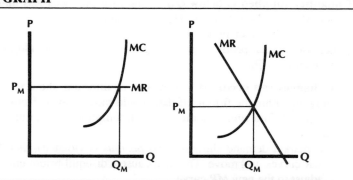

- The graph on the left illustrates the rule for the perfectly competitive firm. With the MR and MC curves shown, profit maximization occurs at output Q_M, at price P_M.
- The graph on the right illustrates the rule for *imperfectly* competitive firms (the sloping MR curve is explained in Key 77). With the MR and MC curves shown, profit maximization occurs at output Q_M, at price P_M.

Key 71 Equilibrium output

OVERVIEW *Equilibrium output for the firm is at the profit maximization point. If the firm produces at any other output level, profit can be increased by moving to the profit maximization point.*

Assumptions (Keys 10–12): *CetPar, EffMar, PerfInfo, Costless, Instant*

Output equilibrium: A firm's output is in *equilibrium* when the firm has no incentive to increase or decrease production. This occurs at the profit maximization point.
- Refer to the graphs in Key 70, where the profit maximization quantity supplied is shown as Q_M.
- Note that the discussion in this Key applies to all firms, not just those in perfectly competitive markets.

If quantity supplied exceeds Q_M: If the firm produces more than Q_M, then *MC* will exceed *MR* for all units in excess of Q_M. The cost (*MC*) of these units is more than the firm will gain in revenue from them (*MR*). The firm loses money on them, and its profit is reduced. The firm can increase profit by eliminating these units, and reducing its quantity supplied to Q_M.

If quantity supplied is below Q_M: If the firm produces less than Q_M, then *MC* will be less than *MR* for additional units produced up to Q_M. The firm can make marginal profit on these units and so increase its total profit by producing them. The firm should increase production to Q_M.

Why changes can occur: If a firm is in equilibrium, there is nothing going on within the firm itself that should move it away from its output equilibrium *unless* some of the assumptions of the model are violated.
- If market demand shifts (*ceteris paribus* is violated), then firms' *MR* curves will move. This will cause a disequilibrium until firms adjust to the new *MR* curve.
- If firms do not have *perfect information*, then they may misinterpret market demand, costs of production, etc. This could lead to changes in either (or both of) *MR* and *MC* and require adjustment to achieve equilibrium output.

Key 72   Long-run market equilibrium

OVERVIEW *In perfectly competitive markets, market forces lead firms, in the long run, to produce at the least-cost point where MR = MC = ATC.*

Assumptions (Keys 10–12): *CetPar, EffMar, PerfInfo, Costless, Instant*

Important! Long-run competitive equilibrium deals with the profit-maximizing reasons why firms enter and leave markets. This means that in addition to the general assumptions listed above, you must remember that in this discussion there are some specific assumptions that are important: 1. Input prices (Theme 10) do not change. 2. Production method, the production function (Key 89), does not change. 3. Market demand does not change.

Long-run equilibrium in perfectly competitive markets: Long-run market equilibrium occurs in perfectly competitive markets when no firms enter or leave the industry. $P_E = MR = MC = ATC$ applies to all firms in the industry in long-run equilibrium. P_E is the long-run market equilibrium price for the output. When market price is at P_E, firms earn normal profit. Remember, normal profit is a *cost* and is included in ATC (Key 16).
- For competitive firms, P_E is the same as MR (Key 71). It is determined in the market by market supply and market demand.
- Market quantity supplied at each price is the sum of what all firms together will supply at that price. Market supply is the sum of all the supply curves (Key 74) of the individual firms.

The graph: The graph on the left is for the individual firm, showing its *ATC* and *MC* curves. The graph on the right is that of the market. *D* is the market demand curve. S_H, S_E, and S_L are different market supply curves. The curve S_E is the long-run equilibrium market supply curve, which yields the equilibrium market price of P_E. Given the assumptions we are working with, the only way a market supply curve can shift in or out is if the number of firms in the market decreases (an inward shift) or increases (an outward shift).

Short-run profits: Suppose the market supply curve is at S_H instead of S_E. Market price will be P_H, which is higher than P_E. Firms will be able to sell their output for more than their *ATC*. This means that their profit will exceed normal profit; they will have *excess profit*. The excess profit per unit of output is $P_H - P_E$. The firm's *total* excess profit is shown by the shaded area in the graph above P_E.

- These excess profits will tempt new entrepreneurs to establish firms in this market, because it is easy to do so and the excess profits are attractive to them.
- When more firms enter the industry, the *market supply curve* will shift outward, resulting in a higher market quantity demanded but at a *lower* market price. New firms will continue to enter the industry until price falls to P_E, the excess profits have been eliminated, the market supply curve is at S_E, and the market is back in long-run equilibrium.

KEY GRAPH

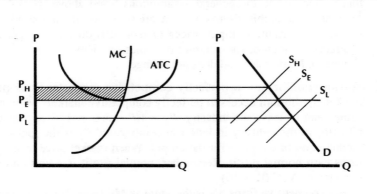

Short-term losses: If market supply is at S_L, then at the market price P_L, firms will not be able to sell their output for as much as ATC; they will sustain *losses*. This has the opposite effect as the reasoning above: firms will *leave* the market to seek better (normal) profits elsewhere. Market supply will shift inward, toward S_E. This process continues until enough firms have left the market to bring market supply back to S_E.

Key 73   The shutdown point

OVERVIEW *If the firm's marginal revenue falls below average cost, the firm will sustain losses. However, there is a range in which it still pays the firm to continue producing. The shutdown point is the point where MR falls below the firm's minimum AVC. At that point the firm's revenues do not cover variable costs, and it will be economic for the firm to cease production and sustain only fixed costs.*

Assumptions (Keys 10–12): *CetPar, EffMar, PerfInfo, Costless, Instant*

The shutdown question: If *MR* falls below *ATC*, the firm earns less than normal profit (sustains abnormal losses) and there is the question of whether to shut the firm down in the short run. Note that if the firm sustains *long-run* abnormal losses, it has time to leave the market completely. Shut-down refers to ceasing production *temporarily, without* leaving the industry.

When *MR* exceeds *AVC*: So long as *MR* exceeds *AVC* (Key 59), the firm should not shut down in the short run. Whether or not the firm produces anything, it sustains its fixed costs. Although the firm is sustaining losses, if *MR* exceeds *AVC*, the firm is covering its variable costs and has revenue left over to apply toward fixed costs. Therefore, if *MR* > *AVC*, the loss is *less* than fixed costs, and the firm should continue to produce.

When *MR* is less than *AVC*: When *MR* falls below the firm's minimum *AVC*, the firm should shut down. If the firm continues to produce, it does not even cover variable costs, so it loses money on *VC* and has to pay *FC* as well. As a result, its loss *exceeds* fixed costs. By shutting down, the firm eliminates all variable costs (when output is 0, *VC* must also be 0). Shutting down *limits* the loss to only the amount of fixed costs.

The shutdown point: The point where *MR = minimum AVC* is the *shutdown point*. At that point, the firm is exactly covering variable costs and the amount of the firm's loss is its fixed cost.

Short and long run: If we relax the *"Costless"* assumption (Key 12), the costs of shutting down and starting up again in the short run may exceed the temporary losses while *MR < AVC*. If so, the firm should not shut down in the short run.

Key 74 MC as the short-run supply curve

OVERVIEW *The portion of the perfectly competitive firm's marginal cost curve above the shutdown point is the firm's short-run supply curve. This does not apply in imperfect competition.*

Assumptions (Keys 10–12): *CetPar, EffMar, PerfInfo, Costless, Instant*

Equilibrium output is on the firm's *MC* curve: The perfectly competitive firm's equilibrium is at the point where $MC = MR = P$ (Key 68).
- The firm's *MR* curve (the market price, *P*) is not under its control and can move about as market conditions change.
- In the short run, as long as input prices don't change (see Theme 10 for discussion of when they *do*), the firm's *MC* curve stays put.
- Since all short-run equilibrium points possible for the firm require that $MC = P$, it follows that they all will be on the firm's *MC* curve.

KEY GRAPH

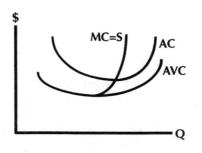

The firm's *MC* curve above *AVC* is the firm's short-run supply curve: The firm's short-run supply curve can be said to be the portion of its *MC* curve above minimum *AVC* (the shutdown point, Key 73).
- A firm's supply curve shows only those equilibrium points at which the firm actually is willing to produce.
- At any point on its *MC* curve *below AVC* the firm shuts down rather than produce anything. Since it won't produce (supply) anything at those points, they aren't part of its supply curve.
- It follows, then, that the perfectly competitive firm's supply curve is its *MC* curve *above AVC*.

Theme 9   IMPERFECT COMPETITION

*I*mperfect competition occurs when the stringent requirements of perfectly competitive markets cannot be met. Specifically, if one or more firms in the industry is large enough to affect the market, or if there is product differentiation among firms, then an imperfectly competitive market exists. Monopoly is a market in which there is only one firm. Monopolistic competition is a market that can have many firms but in which there is product differentiation. Oligopoly refers to markets with relatively few firms, one or more of which is large enough to influence, or even dominate, the market. In markets where there is limited (or no) competition, it may be possible for firms to price-discriminate—to charge different prices to different customers.

Key 75   Monopoly

OVERVIEW *A monopoly is a market that contains a single firm that provides its entire quantity supplied. A natural monopoly is an industry in which a single firm can be more efficient than two or more smaller ones could be. Most forms of monopoly are regulated and/or protected by government.*

Assumptions (Keys 10–12): *CetPar, EffMar, PerfInfo, Costless, Instant*

Monopoly defined: A pure monopoly is an industry with a single firm that produces the market's entire quantity supplied.

Advantages of monopoly to the firm: Monopoly has several advantages from the firm's point of view, the major one being, of course, that there is no other competing firm in the market. The monopolist is able to exert considerable control over both quantity supplied and prices in the market. This creates opportunity for excess profits. A monopoly, then, can be more profitable than a firm in a competitive market (Keys 68–72).

Conditions supporting monopoly: A number of conditions are necessary, or at least desirable, for monopoly.
- *Very difficult entry:* Monopolistic markets require significant entry barriers to keep potential competitors out (Key 67). A common one is *very high cost of entry.*
- *Economies of scale:* Monopolies usually have significant economies of scale, which favor establishment of very large firms because of the potential cost efficiency.
- *Governmental barriers:* Government protects certain monopoly situations with *patents, franchises,* etc.
- *No substitutes:* There should be no close substitutes for the monopolist's product; the fewer poor substitutes, the better. If substitutes exist, then the monopoly position has little advantage because buyers can always switch to the substitute.
- *Inelastic demand for product:* This is not absolutely necessary, but it helps and is a feature of most monopolistic markets. This is because elastic demand often means that substitutes are available.
- *Natural monopoly:* Some industries, for various reasons, can operate more efficiently as monopolies than as competitive markets. These are termed *natural monopolies* (Key 110).

Key 76   Monopoly: Demand, TR, and MR

OVERVIEW *The monopolist's demand curve is the market demand curve; it slopes downward. Because of this, the monopolist's marginal revenue curve also slopes downward.*

Assumptions (Keys 10–12): *CetPar, EffMar, PerfInfo, Costless, Instant*

The monopolist's demand curve: The monopolistic firm sees its demand curve as the market's demand curve, as shown in the diagram.

The monopolist's marginal revenue curve: *Warning!* The monopolist's *MR* curve is one of the trickier aspects of economic theory for the student to grasp.

- Recall that *MR* is the change in total revenue experienced by a firm when it increases output by one unit (Key 69). Since the monopolist faces a downward-sloping *D* curve, it must *reduce price* on *all* its output in order to sell each marginal unit, assuming that price discrimination (Key 86) among its consumers is not possible.

- Therefore, *MR* is not the full amount that the marginal unit sells for. That amount *must be reduced* by revenue *lost* by reducing the price on all the *other* units being sold.

KEY GRAPH

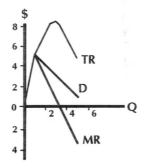

Example: The table below shows hypothetical data used to generate the graph:

Q	P	TR	MR
1	5	5	5
2	4	8	3
3	3	9	1
4	2	8	-1
5	1	5	-3

- As Q increases, P falls. *MR* is positive but *falling*, for the reasons described above.
- *TR* increases, but at a decreasing rate, since MR is falling. Eventually *TR* peaks and then begins to fall. At this point, *MR* becomes *negative*.

Key 77   Monopoly: Equilibrium output

OVERVIEW *Like any other firm, the monopolist produces the quantity at which MR = MC. Because of the monopolist's downward sloping demand and MR curves, equilibrium price is not the same as MR or ATC. Therefore, the MC curve is not the monopolist's supply curve.*

Assumptions (Keys 10–12): *CetPar, EffMar, PerfInfo, Costless, Instant*

Equilibrium under monopoly: The monopolist's equilibrium (profit maximization) point is the quantity at which $MR = MC$.
- In the graph, $MC = MR$ at point E. Quantity supplied is Q_M, price is P_M.
- The downward-sloping MR curve is *not* the same as P_M (Key 78). Therefore, at equilibrium output, P_M exceeds ATC, which exceeds MR. They are not equal.

KEY GRAPH

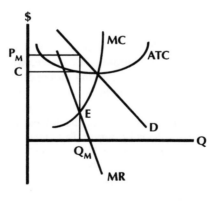

MC **is not the monopolist's supply curve:** MC is not the monopolist's supply curve, because the firm does not produce where $MC = P_M$. Usually it produces at a point where MC is less than P_M, so while Q_M is on the MC curve, the P_M associated with each Q_M is not. Since the firm's supply curve illustrates the relationship between Q_M and P_M, the supply curve necessarily must lie somewhere different from the competitive firm's MC curve.

Key 78 Monopoly profits and inefficiency

OVERVIEW *Due to its downward sloping demand and MR curves, the monopolist's equilibrium output usually results in excess profits, because equilibrium price is usually higher than average total cost.*

Assumptions (Keys 10–12): *CetPar, EffMar, PerfInfo, Costless, Instant*

Monopoly profits: Refer to the graph in Key 77. The monopolist is the only firm in the market, and entry and exit in the market is very difficult for other firms. Therefore, there is no competitive pressure (other firms entering and exiting the market) to drive the monopolist to produce at the point where $MC = ATC$.

- In the graph, at the equilibrium quantity supplied Q_M, ATC is C, which is less than the market price P_M.
- Since normal profit (Key 16) is included in ATC and the monopolist's ATC is *less* than the market price, the firm has *excess profit* of $P_M - C$ per unit of output.
- Because of the nature of monopoly, such excess profits are common and usually can be sustained indefinitely. Economists refer to excess profits of monopoly as *monopoly profits*.

Inefficiency of monopoly: For the monopolist, market price of the output is P_M. This is higher than MC, and higher than ATC. Furthermore, due to the sloping MR curve, which lies below the demand curve, the profit-maximizing monopolist produces less than the quantity where ATC would be at its lowest point.

- The monopolist may be technically and economically efficient (Key 65) in that it produces at the lowest possible cost for its *profit-maximizing level of output.* But since the monopolist's output is less than the level of lowest ATC and since its ATC is higher than the lowest possible ATC, the monopolist is not *allocatively* efficient (Key 65).
- Note that many economists suggest that this may not always be all that bad in the real world. Although monopolists do not produce at the lowest points on their ATC curves, the large sizes of monopolistic firms may lead to economies of scale (Key 63) that yield lower costs, even with monopoly profits, than could be achieved in a market composed of several smaller firms.

Key 79   Monopolistic competition:

D and MR

OVERVIEW *Monopolistic competition describes a competitive market in which the firms do not produce homogeneous output.*

Assumptions (Keys 10–12): *CetPar, EffMar, PerfInfo, Costless, Instant*

Monopolistic competition: *Monopolistic competition* resembles perfect competition (Keys 68–72) in that there is a large number of firms in the industry and there are few barriers to entry or exit (Key 67). Therefore, individual firms *cannot influence the market.* Output is distinguished by *product differentiation* (Key 66). It is *not* homogeneous from firm to firm, but each firm's output is a *close substitute* for the product of the others.

D and MR: Because of product differentiation, the firm perceives downward-sloping market demand for its output, with a downward-sloping *MR* curve below the *D* curve. (The reasoning is the same as that in Key 77 for monopoly.)
- Since products are close substitutes, many, but not all buyers will substitute another product as the firm's output price rises. If the firm's price falls, it attracts buyers from other firms.
- Therefore, quantity demanded for the monopolistically competitive firm's product changes rapidly as its price changes. As a result, the firm's demand curve and *MR* curve are quite elastic, though different and not perfectly elastic.

KEY GRAPH

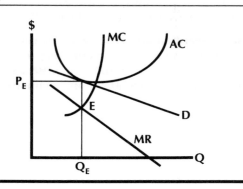

Key 80   Monopolistic competition:

Market equilibrium

OVERVIEW *Monopolistically competitive firms produce where price and ATC are equal so there is no excess profit. However, they do not produce where MR = ATC, so they do not achieve least-cost production.*

Assumptions (Keys 10–12): *CetPar, EffMar, PerfInfo, Costless, Instant*

Market equilibrium under monopolistic competition: Refer to the graph in Key 79. The firm produces at the quantity where $MR = MC$. This is quantity supplied Q_E and price P_E. Competition also will assure that $P_E = ATC$. This is due to the ease of entry and exit and the close substitutability of firms' output in the monopolistically competitive market (Key 79).

- If firms in such a market are showing excess profits (P_E exceeds ATC), it is easy for new firms to enter the market seeking the higher profits.
- The new firms produce close substitutes for existing firms' products. Therefore, they compete closely (though not perfectly) with the others, and their entry into the market shifts all firms' demand curves inward (Key 28).
- This, in turn, shifts firms' MR curves inward and reduces excess profit. New firms will continue to enter the market until the excess profit has been eliminated. This can happen only when $P_E = ATC$ and $MR = MC$.
- If there are *too many* firms in the market, ATC will be above D (and therefore P_E) at all points, and firms will have losses. This will encourage some firms to leave the market; demand curves for remaining firms will shift outward until $P_E = ATC$.

Monopolistic competition and efficiency: Though monopolistically competitive firms have no excess profits, they do not achieve least-cost production (where $MC = MR = AC$). Because of downward sloping demand and MR, the $MR = MC$ equilibrium is not at the lowest ATC.

Key 81 Oligopoly

OVERVIEW *Oligopoly is an imperfectly competitive market in which entry may be difficult and at least some firms are large enough to influence the market. A key element of oligopoly theory is that firms base their actions, at least in part, upon their perception of what other firms in the industry will do. Oligopoly can be quite complex. Introductory economics texts consider three types: collusion, price leadership, and the kinked-demand model.*

Assumptions (Keys 10–12): *CetPar, EffMar, PerfInfo, Costless, Instant*

Characteristics of oligopoly: *Oligopoly* is an imperfect market in which there are competing firms but the industry is dominated by at least one firm large enough to influence the market. There may be product differentiation. Entry and exit are difficult, usually because of the huge investment required to establish a viably competitive new firm.

Mutual interdependence: An important feature of oligopolistic firms is that they base their actions, at least in part, upon their perception of how the industry's *other* firms will react to anything they do. Economists refer to this as *mutual interdependence*.

Three kinds of oligopoly: Introductory economics texts usually discuss three variations of oligopoly.
- *Collusion* occurs when firms conspire to fix prices and (sometimes) each firm's market share. The objective of collusion is to eliminate competitive effects, so that the entire industry can act as though it were a single *monopoly*, and enjoy monopoly profits. When collusion is successful, its results are the same as for monopoly (Keys 75–78).
- The *price leadership model* (Key 83) features a dominant firm whose pricing decisions are followed by the industry's other firms, but without an overt price-fixing agreement. Some firms in this model may be quite small, but the price-leading firm is large.
- The *kinked-demand model* (Keys 84–85) describes an industry with several large firms that make pricing decisions independently. Each firm's decision-making assumes that all the other firms will match any price reductions but will not match any price increases.

Key 82   Oligopoly: Demand and MR

OVERVIEW *Oligopolistic firms experience a downward-sloping demand curve and MR curve.*

Assumptions (Keys 10–12): *CetPar, EffMar, PerfInfo, Costless, Instant*

Demand and marginal revenue for the large oligopolistic firm: In any oligopoly, at least one firm is so large that its actions will have an effect upon the market; often there may be several such large firms. Just as in monopoly, these large firms perceive a *downward-sloping* market demand for their output. Therefore, they also experience the downward sloping marginal revenue curve that lies *below* the demand curve. The explanation is the same as that shown for monopoly in Key 76.

The small firm in oligopolistic markets: Oligopoly allows for small firms in its markets; all that is necessary is that at least one firm be large. So far as the small firms are concerned, the large firms are price leaders (Key 83); it is their action that determines the market price.
- The small firms are too small to affect the market and are price takers in that they follow the leader's pricing.
- Therefore, they perceive their demand and *MR* to be perfectly elastic, just like the perfectly competitive firm (Keys 68–72).
- The small firms may appear efficient in that they may also produce where the market price equals their *MC* and *ATC*. However, in many oligopolistic industries economists have observed that the larger firms actually produce at lower cost than the smaller ones due to economies of scale (Key 63).

Inefficiency of the large oligopolistic firm: Since large oligopolistic firms face a downward-sloping demand curve, they do not produce at the least-cost point (lowest *ATC*). The reasoning is the same as explained in the discussion of monopoly (Key 78).
- These large oligopolistic firms, then, do not produce at the lowest point on their *ATC* curves and so have excess profit. Thus, they do not achieve least-cost production and are inefficient.
- Note from the discussion above, though, that the size of these firms may lead to economies of scale that result in lower costs than smaller firms.

Key 83   Oligopoly: Price leadership

OVERVIEW *The price leadership model of oligopoly describes an industry dominated by a single firm. Its pricing decisions are followed by the other firms in the industry.*

Assumptions (Keys 10–12): *CetPar, EffMar, PerfInfo, Costless, Instant*

Price leadership model: This model describes an industry dominated by a single large firm, though there are other, much smaller firms as well.

- The dominant firm usually benefits from economies of scale and so could drive the smaller ones out of business by price-cutting until they all fail.
- It "allows" the other firms to remain, usually to avoid government interference such as anti-trust action.

Pricing behavior: The dominant firm makes its profit-maximizing pricing decisions; the smaller firms follow suit. This complicated-looking graph describes price leadership.

KEY GRAPH

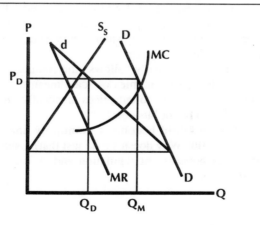

- The market demand curve is *DD*. The *cumulative* (all of them together) supply curve for the *small* firms in the market is S_S.

Dominant firm's demand and marginal revenue: The dominant firm derives its perceived demand curve (d) by subtracting the cumulative supply S_S of all the smaller firms from the market demand curve DD.

- From its downward-sloping market demand d, the dominant firm derives its own marginal revenue curve (MR).
- The dominant firm's MR is downward-sloping, and lies below the firm's demand curve d. The reasoning for this is the same as for monopoly (Key 76).

Equilibrium under price leadership: The dominant firm produces its own quantity supplied of Q_D, which is determined by the intersection of its MR and MC curves.

- This results in price P_D, as determined by the dominant firm's demand curve (d).
- At this price, quantity demanded in the market is Q_M, which is more than the dominant firm's output of Q_D.
- The difference between the two ($Q_M - Q_D$) is the quantity supplied by all the smaller firms together.
- The smaller firms also receive price P_D for their output.

Results of price leadership: The effect of price leadership is that the dominant firm makes its pricing decision based upon its own profit maximization situation: $MR = MC$.

- None of the small firms is large enough to have a significant effect upon the market by itself. Thus, the small firms' MR and equilibrium are similar to perfectly competitive firms (Key 69) in that they "accept" the price leader's price and so perceive a perfectly elastic $MR = P_D$ curve.
- The dominant firm usually "allows" the smaller firms to remain in the industry. Its economies of scale mean that the dominant firm usually can afford to cut prices drastically until the smaller firms are driven out of business.
- If it did so, it could become a monopoly and enjoy higher monopoly profits. Why doesn't it do just that? Usually because of the threat of government regulation and/or intervention (Keys 109, 110, 111).

Key 84   Oligopoly: Kinked demand

OVERVIEW *The kinked-demand model of oligopoly describes an industry dominated by a few large firms. Their pricing behavior assumes that other firms will match any price decrease the firm implements but will not match price increases.*

Assumptions (Keys 10–12): *CetPar, EffMar, PerfInfo, Costless, Instant*

KEY GRAPH

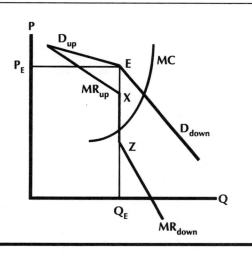

Kinked-demand model: This model of oligopoly considers industries that are dominated by more than one large firm. The key difference here is the manner in which firms are assumed to react to *other* firms' pricing decisions.

- Each firm assumes that if it raises its price, other firms *will not raise their prices*. Instead, each of them will keep its lower price to capture market share from the price-raising firm.
- Each firm assumes that if it lowers its price, other firms *will match the price decrease*. They will do so in order to avoid losing market share to the price-lowering firm.

    Firms therefore perceive two sets of demand and *MR* curves: one for when they increase prices and one for when they reduce prices. These are explained further in Key 85.

Key 85   Kinked demand:

Market equilibrium

OVERVIEW *Market prices in kinked-demand oligopoly tend to be very "sticky."*

Assumptions (Keys 10–12): *CetPar, EffMar, PerfInfo, Costless, Instant*

Graphical representation: Refer to the graph in Key 84. Since the firm expects different behavior from its competitors depending upon whether it raises or lowers price, it perceives a *different* market demand curve for each situation.

- If the firm *raises* its price, it does *not* expect competitors to go along and it sees *elastic* market demand; buyers will likely substitute competitors' cheaper goods and the firm will lose market share. See the elastic curve D_{up} in the graph.
- If the firm *lowers* its price, it expects competitors to *match* its action and it sees more *inelastic* demand. Other firms' price-matching will prevent the firm from capturing market share from them. See the inelastic curve D_{down} in the graph.
- The two demand curves "meet" at the point E where the firm is producing. They appear to the firm as a single market demand curve which is "kinked" at point E.

Marginal revenue: Each of the two perceived demand curves has its own *MR* curve (MR_{up} and MR_{down}), which apply in the same relevant area as the demand curves from which they are derived. However, because of the way *MR* curves are derived from downward-sloping demand curves (Key 76), the two *MR* curves *do not* overlap or meet. This creates a "mathematically undefined" area between points X and Z : it is not on either *MR* curve.

Equilibrium output: The firm produces the output at the point where $MR = MC$; price is P_E. As long as *MC* intersects anywhere on XZ, the firm will remain in equilibrium.

- The *MC* curve can move about quite a bit within the XZ area without changing Q_E or P_E, so prices in this form of oligopoly tend to be very "sticky." It takes a considerable change in the firm's cost structure to make a price change profitable.
- If, however, the firm should achieve a new equilibrium at a different price and quantity supplied, the "kink" in the demand curve (and the two *MR* curves) would move as well. The kink always occurs at the firm's equilibrium output level.

Key 86   Price discrimination

OVERVIEW *The object of price discrimination is to control the price that individual customers pay so as to increase the firm's profits by obtaining some of the consumer surplus.*

Assumptions (Keys 10–12): *Ceteris paribus*

Price discrimination: *Price discrimination* occurs when a firm is able to charge different prices to different customers and there is no cost difference to the firm of supplying the different customers.

Price differentials: Price discrimination is not the same thing as *price differentials*. Price differentials reflect lower or higher costs to firms of transacting business with certain customers. *Examples:* charging transportation costs to the buyer, volume discounts (lower transaction costs for the firm).

Conditions for successful price discrimination: To be successful, price discrimination requires a number of conditions. Remember, the objective is to be able to force different buyers to pay different prices for the same good. If this can be done, the firm can secure some of the consumer surplus (Key 48) from at least some of its customers.
*   *A good for which there are no viable substitutes*: If there are good substitutes for the firm's output, then price-discriminated customers will avoid the price discrimination by buying substitutes from other firms.
*   *Monopoly or equivalent*: The seller must be able to control price. In nonmonopoly situations, there are competitors who can sell at lower prices, unless all sellers *collude* (Key 81) to enforce price discrimination throughout the market.
*   *Different elasticities*: The market for the seller's good can be segregated into sets of customers with different elasticities of demand. Price discrimination will work best against those customers with inelastic demand, since they can be charged higher prices with little loss of quantity demanded, and the firm will achieve higher *TR* from them.
*   *Customer segregation*: The firm must have a way to *segregate* its customers from one another, to keep them from trading among themselves. Otherwise, customers who buy cheaply can resell to those who have to pay the higher price and so defeat the firm's attempt at price discrimination.

Key 87   Examples of price discrimination

OVERVIEW   *Examples of price discrimination include some utility rates, airline fare structures, and certain international trade practices.*

Assumptions (Keys 10–12): *Ceteris paribus*

Price discrimination: Price discrimination is practiced in a variety of situations in today's economy.

Utility rates: Utility companies usually are regulated *natural monopolies* (Key 110). Their product is difficult for consumers to resell among themselves, and it has no (or only very poor) substitutes. Demand elasticity usually is high.
- Utilities can price-discriminate by charging different rates for usage at different times of day (not necessarily true price discrimination, since cost differentials may be involved), and by separating their customers into different rate groups such as households, businesses, etc.
- Utilities produce output that customers cannot easily trade among themselves. It is difficult or impossible for those who pay lower rates to hoard such products as electricity, gas, phone service, etc., and sell them to others.

Airline fares: The airline industry has few competitors, and price leadership is prevalent. Some airlines also have near-monopolies in some markets. Thus, substitution is not easy for buyers.
- Airlines usually charge lower fares to passengers who book and pay fares well in advance; they are price-discriminating against those who must travel on short notice.
- Passengers who buy cheaper tickets ahead of time can conceivably resell their tickets later to other travelers, but it is difficult for them to get together and make the trade. Also, airlines sometimes police ticketing and refuse to honor tickets that have been traded.

International trade: With the cooperation of their governments, firms in some countries charge different prices for domestic sales than for international sales. Since it is difficult for customers to trade across international barriers and long distances, this can be very effective. Also, governments can impose domestic regulations preventing imports from foreigners who purchased the goods at a lower price.

Theme 10   PRODUCTION AND
INPUT MARKETS

*I*nput markets are those in which firms acquire the factors of production that they employ in the production process. The firm is faced with costs of inputs as determined by input markets. It then must allocate its use of these various inputs so as to maximize its profits. To do this, it equates the marginal product of each input with the price of the input as given in the input market. Input markets sometimes feature monopsony (a single buyer) and the equivalent of monopoly in the form of labor unions.

Key 88   Inputs, factors of production

OVERVIEW *Inputs are the resources firms must buy and use to produce output. They are among the classical economic factors of production: land, labor, and capital.*

Inputs: All production processes must buy and use resources of various kinds in order to operate and produce output. Resources used by firms in this manner are called *inputs*. Inputs sometimes are called *factors of production*. Generally, however, when economists refer to factors of production, they refer to the "classical" large categories of *land, labor,* and *capital*. A few economists also consider *entrepreneurship* to be a factor of production.

- *Land* is required because there has to be someplace to put the production enterprise; also, it is a significant input in agricultural enterprise. To economists of previous centuries, in whose day agriculture was much more dominant than in today's industrial economy, land was considered a more important input than it is to today's economists. The return to land (what it is paid) is called *rent* (Keys 97, 98).
- *Labor* is required in order to operate the process and to perform many functions that other inputs cannot. The return to labor (what it is paid) is *wages*; to acquire labor, entrepreneurs must pay the market wage for the labor they buy. Households are the suppliers of labor.
- Modern economies are technologically advanced; they use factories, machinery, tools, etc. All of this productive equipment is called *capital*, or *capital equipment*. The return to capital is called *interest*.

Entrepreneurship: Entrepreneurship is described in Key 16. Its return is *profit*. In competitive markets, the return to entrepreneurship is *normal profit*. Entrepreneurship itself is not usually considered an input, because its function is to gather and manage all the other inputs into a production process.

Key 89   Production functions

OVERVIEW *A production function shows the relationship among combinations of factors of production and the maximum outputs they can be used to produce.*

Assumptions (Keys 10–12): *Ceteris paribus*

Production function: Production functions usually are shown as mathematical expressions relating combinations of variable inputs and the maximum output they can produce: $Q_S = f(a, b, c,...)$, where a, b, c, etc., are inputs. This is a formal way of saying that if the amounts of variable inputs used in a production process are changed, the quantity of output will change in a certain way.
- Any input whose amount used can be changed in the short run is a *variable input*.
- Production functions can be very complex or very simple. The simplest show the changes in Q_S due to varying the amount of a single variable input.

Example: An entrepreneur opens a photocopying shop. The variable input to be considered is *labor*. The copy machines, the building, etc., all are fixed equipment; they are not variable inputs. The production function, relating output (Q_S) to the quantity of labor used is shown in the table below. It is shown graphically as *TP* in the graph in Key 90.
- The entrepreneur hires one person ($L = 1$) who has to operate the machines, serve customers, take payments, etc. If hiring that one person allows the shop to produce 2000 copies a day, the production function shows that when $L = 1$, $Q_S = 2000$.
- A second person is hired ($L = 2$). Now someone can always be on at least one of the copying machines, and customers can be served more quickly. Output (Q_S) rises to 5000 copies a day: When $L = 2$, $Q_S = 5000$. As a third and fourth person are hired, Q_S rises to 7500 and 9000 copies, respectively.
- The table also shows average product (AP_L) and marginal physical product (MPP_L) of labor, described in Key 90.

L	Q_s	AP_L	MPP_L
1	2000	2000	2000
2	5000	2500	3000
3	7500	2500	2500
4	9000	2250	1500

Key 90   Marginal physical product

OVERVIEW *Marginal physical product is used to determine the equilibrium in input markets.*

Assumptions (Keys 10–12): *Ceteris paribus*

Marginal physical product: *Marginal physical product* (*MPP*) is the additional output obtained from using one additional unit of a variable input. $MPP_I = \Delta Q_S / \Delta I$, where Q_S is the quantity supplied and I is a variable input.

- In the photocopy shop example (Key 89) when one unit of labor (one person) was hired, output was 2000 copies a day. MPP_L of that first unit of labor is 2000. Hiring a second person increased output to 5000. MPP_L of that second unit of labor is the additional 3000 units of output.
- Eventually, the increasing variable input crowds fixed inputs. Diminishing returns (Key 56) sets in, and *MPP* begins to fall. This is because only the specific input being observed is varying; *everything else stays the same.* In the example in Key 89, diminishing returns sets in after two people are hired, and MPP_L falls thereafter. MPP_L falls to 2500 for the third unit of labor and 1500 for the fourth.

KEY GRAPH

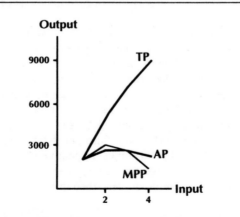

Average product, total product: *AP* is the mean quantity of output produced by a variable input (see table in Key 89). *TP* in the graph shows Q_S at different quantities of input. The *TP* curve, also, is the graph of the production function (Key 89).

Key 91   Marginal revenue product

OVERVIEW *Marginal revenue product of a variable input is the additional revenue that a firm receives from selling the marginal product provided by the use of one additional unit of that input.*

Assumptions (Keys 10–12): *Ceteris paribus*

Marginal revenue product (MRP): The *marginal revenue product (MRP)* is the additional revenue that the firm will receive by selling the marginal physical product (Key 90) provided by one additional unit of a variable input.

- For example, if an additional unit of labor is used, its marginal revenue product (MRP_L) will be the marginal product (MPP_L) of that additional unit multiplied by the firm's marginal revenue (Key 69):

$$MRP_L = MPP_L \times MR$$

- If the firm is a perfect competitor, then MR is the same as the price P_Y that its output brings in the market (Key 68).
- MRP also can be calculated by dividing the change in total revenue (Key 69) by the change in the quantity used of the variable input:

$$MRP_L = \Delta TR\ /\ \Delta L$$

KEY GRAPH

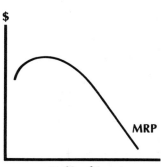

Units of Input

Key 92   Equilibrium of the firm

in input markets

OVERVIEW *The firm achieves profit maximizing equilibrium in its use of an input when the MRP of the input is equal to the input's marginal factor cost (MFC).*

Assumptions (Keys 10–12): *Ceteris paribus*

Profit maximization in the use of inputs: It will increase total profits for the firm to use an input, as long as the input's *MRP* (Key 91) exceeds the firm's cost of using it. The cost to the firm of using an input I is the firm's *marginal factor cost (MFC$_I$)* for that input.
- So long as MRP_I exceeds MFC_I, it costs the firm less to use the input than it makes by selling the *MPP* (Key 90) it can produce by using the input.
- This will be true until the point where MRP_I equals the firm's cost of the input, MFC_I. Therefore, the equilibrium position of the firm in the use of input I is the point where $MRP_I = MFC_I$.
- For a firm in perfect competition, $MFC_I = P_I$, the price of the input in the market.

Graph: In the graph, P_I is the market price of input I. MRP_I is the marginal revenue product for this input when used by the firm. The firm will use quantity Q_I of the input.

KEY GRAPH

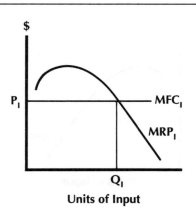

Key 93   Multiple inputs

OVERVIEW *Firms that use more than one input should use each one so that MRP_I / MFC_I is the same for all inputs.*

Assumptions (Keys 10–12): *Ceteris paribus*

Firms using more than one input: Most firms use more than a single input. (The photocopy store in Key 89, for example, can rent more machines as well as hire more labor.) The profit maximization situation is similar to the one-input model (Key 92).
- The firm should use inputs so that $MRP_I = MFC_I$ for all inputs:

$$MRP_J = MFC_J; \; MRP_K = MFC_K; \; MRP_L = MFC_L; \text{ etc.}$$

- By algebraic manipulation, and by considering that $MFC_I = P_I$ for most firms, we can rewrite the above:

$$MPP_J / P_J = MPP_K / P_K = MPP_L / P_L$$

- In other words, the marginal physical product *per dollar spent* on inputs should be the same for all inputs.

Changes in input prices and substitution of inputs: Any change in the price of an input will affect the value of MPP_I / P_I.
- If P_I rises, then the value of MPP_I / P_I will fall. The firm gets less output per dollar from input I than from other inputs. Therefore, it will be profitable to use less of input I and *substitute* more of the other inputs.
- This will raise the value of MPP_I / P_I, while MPP / P falls for the other inputs, and a new equilibrium will be achieved with the firm using less of I and more of the other inputs.
- A drop in the price of input I has the opposite effect. I will be substituted for some of the other inputs because the higher value for MPP_I / P_I makes it profitable for the firm to do so.

Changes in input prices and the firm's cost and supply curves: Changes in input prices will affect the firm's cost structure and so the firm's supply curve for its output in the output market.
- *Falling* input prices will reduce the firm's costs and shift its output supply curve *outward*; the firm's quantity supplied at each price will be higher.
- *Rising* input prices will have the opposite effect, shifting the firm's output supply curve *inward*.

Key 94   Monopsony

OVERVIEW   *Monopsony is the situation where there is one single buyer (the monopsonist) in the market. In the real world, it appears only in some input markets.*

Assumptions (Keys 10–12): *Ceteris paribus*

Marginal factor cost in monopsony: Most firms are *price takers* in input markets, facing perfectly elastic supply where $MFC_I = P_I$.
- The monopsonist, however, is the only buyer in an input market. It faces an *upward-sloping* market supply curve for the input, so its MFC_I is not equal to P_I, and its MFC_I is not the same at different levels of quantity used of the input.
- Monopsony occurs mostly in input markets, where big firms can dominate.

Graphical depiction: The graph below shows a monopsonistic market for labor. W is the wage rate. S_L is the market supply curve of labor; MFC_L is the marginal factor cost curve of labor facing the monopsonist. MRP_L is the monopsonist's marginal revenue product of labor; it is derived as in Key 91. Since the monopsonist faces the upward-sloping market supply curve of labor, using more labor leads to an increase in the price paid for all units of labor used. Therefore, MFC_L will lie above S_L.

KEY GRAPH

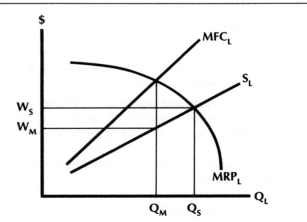

Equilibrium in monopsony: Just as in Key 93, the monopsonist uses inputs up to the point where $MFC_L = MRP_L$. However, since the monopsonist's MFC_L curve is not the same as the S_L curve, it will use less input, at a lower input price, than the firm which competes in input markets.

- In a labor market where firms compete as input buyers, the equilibrium market wage would be W_S and the quantity of labor demanded/supplied would be Q_S. (This is determined by the intersection of S_L with MRP_L.)

- In a monopsonistic labor market with a single input buyer, the equilibrium wage would be lower (W_M) and the quantity demanded/supplied of labor lower (S_M). This happens because the monopsonist's equilibrium in the labor market is determined by the intersection of MRP_L with MFC_L, and *not* with S_L.

Inefficiency of monopsony: In the situation described above, W_M is considerably below MRP_L. Although MRP_L is the actual "value" to society of the productivity of labor, the W_M that the monopsonist pays for labor is lower. Since the monopsonist's equilibrium is below the point where $MRP_L = S_L$, some labor whose MRP_L would exceed its price is not used. Since this unused labor could be more productive here than in some alternative employment, monopsony is inefficient.

Remedies for monopsony: Remedies for monopsony can involve government or private action.

- A *minimum wage*, set at W_S, will create a perfectly elastic supply curve to that point. Over that range, therefore, MFC_L would be the same as W_S, and the monopsonist would hire up to the competitive equilibrium point. (The catch, of course, is that government has to be able to determine exactly what W_S really is: setting a minimum wage at any other level would still be inefficient, though possibly less so than allowing the monopsonist to operate totally unregulated.)

- *Labor unions* (Key 95) act on behalf of the entire supply side of the input market for labor. Their objective is to create the equivalent of a monopoly on the supply side. The effect in the market would be a powerful monopsonist facing a powerful monopolist. The market result (eventual W and Q_L) would depend upon the relative powers of the two.

Key 95 Labor unions and collective bargaining

OVERVIEW *Labor unions came into being in the United States after a long struggle, as a means of confronting powerful quasi-monopsonistic employers with a united front of equivalent power. In markets where unions are significant, the competitive market process is replaced with collective bargaining, wherein the union contracts with employers on behalf of all workers.*

History of organized labor: Organized labor (unions) originated in the U.S. in the late 19th century, in response to monopsonistic domination of labor markets by monopolistic firms and collusion (trusts) between firms. Growth in membership increased rapidly in the 1930s and 1940s; since the mid-1950s, union membership as a percent of U.S. employed has declined from about 35% to less than 20%.
  * The *Knights of Labor*, founded in 1869, was the first successful labor union, but its radical policies eventually led to its decline.
  * The *American Federation of Labor* (AFL) was founded in 1881 as a nonideological organization. Its objective was the organization of skilled labor.
  * In 1935 the *National Labor Relations Act* was passed by the U.S. government. It guarantees workers the right to join a union and requires employers to engage in *collective bargaining* (negotiate only with the union about pay and working conditions) if a majority of their employees want them to.
  * The *Congress of Industrial Organizations* (CIO) was founded in 1935 by a rebellious group of AFL affiliated unions. Competition between AFL and CIO led to increased labor organization effort, and union membership grew rapidly until about 1950.
  * AFL and CIO merged in 1955.

Decline of union membership: Union membership, as a percent of those employed, has fallen by about half since the 1950s.
  * Some analysts suggest that the union movement has been the victim of its own success: legislation protecting the rights of all workers, minimum-wage laws, child-labor laws, etc., all have been the result of pressure by organized labor but, at the same time, have lessened many workers' perception of their need for union organization.

- Some "excesses" by powerful unions (restricting membership, forcing employers to hire extraneous workers, etc.) may also have served to tarnish the labor movement's image.
- In many markets, foreign competition (which may use much less expensive labor) has made it more difficult for unions to maintain high wages and employment.
- Deregulation of many industries in the 1970s and 1980s (Key 111) has given rise to new nonunion firms that compete effectively with unionized ones.

Economics of unions: The objective of the union is to act as a monopolist in the input market. As a result, it may be able to produce monopoly profits (Key 78) for its members.
- The most effective way to do this is to restrict membership to a level lower than equilibrium supply would be in a competitive market. This results in a higher wage rate for union members than would exist in a competitive market.
- This, of course, is economically inefficient. Some labor, even though its *MRP* would exceed its *MFC*, would be unemployed or employed elsewhere with a lower value of marginal product. However, the unemployed labor would not be members of the union; the union, therefore, would be benefiting its members.
- Unions also present a united front for workers against potentially powerful monopsonistic employers. Referring to the graph in Key 94, if unions set a wage of W_S, they actually would promote a more efficient allocation of resources. It is when they manage to negotiate a wage *greater* than W_S that they obtain monopoly profits for their members.

Key 96   Backward-bending
supply curve of labor

OVERVIEW   *Labor is supplied by households. While the supply offered depends upon the wage rate, households also must consider the opportunity cost of giving up leisure when they supply labor. It is possible that if the wage rate rises high enough, quantity supplied of labor actually will fall because workers will substitute leisure for some of the high wage that they could be getting.*

Assumptions (Keys 10–12): *Ceteris paribus*

Household supply of labor: The household is the supplier of labor in the labor input market. To the household, there is a trade-off between leisure and working (supplying labor).
- *Leisure*, in economics, is defined as any time spent in *nonlabor* activities. This can include play, vacations, TV viewing, entertainment (things we normally would think of as leisure) but also includes *everything else* that is nonlabor: chores, child-rearing, eating, sleeping, being too ill or too old to work, etc.
- Time spent working (supplying labor) produces income, which can be used by the household for consumption. Time spent working also is time lost to leisure. Therefore, the opportunity cost (Key 18) of time spent on leisure is the forgone consumption that would have been paid for by the wages earned if the time had been spent working.

Supply curve of labor: The above discussion suggests that as wages rise, households will supply more labor. This is because at higher wage rates, the opportunity cost of leisure becomes higher.
- When wages are low, the household doesn't give up much consumption by spending more time on leisure (forgoing work). When wages are high, spending time on leisure requires giving up a greater amount of consumption.
- This discussion suggests an upward-sloping supply curve for labor.

Income and substitution effects of wage rate changes: The trade-offs described above are *substitution effects* (Key 45). However, there also is an *income effect* (Key 45) involved that can have unusual results.

- If wages rise, workers can buy more (consume more) without increasing the amount of time they work.
- One of the things they can buy is *more leisure*. This is bought simply by working *less* time.

Example: A worker works 40 hours a week, for $8 per hour; weekly income is $320. If the wage rises to $10 per hour, income rises to $400 per week, with no additional work. The worker is better off and can raise consumption.

- The key point here is that the wage increase means that the worker can choose to have a higher income than before or to work *fewer* hours. The worker "trades" *some* of the wage increase for *more leisure*, i.e., supplies less labor by working fewer hours.
- Suppose the worker decides to work only 36 hours per week at the new higher wage rate. His/her income now would be $360, $40 more than before. *Also*, the worker would have 4 more hours of leisure per week. He/she has chosen to take part of the wage increase in money ($40 more of income) and part in the form of leisure.
- The result is that the increase in the wage has led to *less* labor being supplied, instead of more.

KEY GRAPH

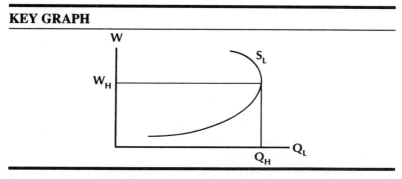

Backward-bending supply curve of labor: At some relatively high wage rate (W_H), the income effect overcomes the substitution effect and workers will prefer to spend part of the higher wage on more leisure. At this point, the supply curve of labor would begin to move backward.

- Quantity of labor supplied, then, would never exceed Q_H, the quantity at which the backward bend occurs.
- Any increase in wage above W_H would lead to a *decrease* in the quantity supplied of labor. The income effect of the higher wage would result in fewer hours worked in return for higher consumption of leisure.

Key 97   Economic rent

OVERVIEW *Economic rent is the portion of the return to a factor of production that exceeds the minimum amount necessary to bring it into use.*

Rent: To economists the term *rent* has a very special meaning. (It comes from Ricardo's theory of land *rent,* described in Key 98.) Rent is the portion of the payment to an input that exceeds the minimum amount necessary to bring it into use.

Warning! The concept of economic rent (perhaps due partly to its odd name) is a difficult one for the beginning economics student to grasp. Make sure you understand it.

Example: Joe is a talented baseball player. His salary is $1 million a year, determined in a competitive market: teams bid for his services, and he plays for the one willing to pay him the most. If Joe did not play baseball, the next best work he could do would be to sell cars for $50,000 per year.
- Therefore, it can be argued that he should be willing to play baseball for no more than $50,001 per year. At that salary, baseball would pay him more than any *other* work he could do. As an *economic man* (Key 12), Joe's rational action is to play baseball for *any* salary above $50,000.
- The *economic rent* that Joe earns playing baseball, then, is $949,999. This is the amount in *excess* of the $50,001 that would be "enough" to get Joe to play baseball.

Rent as a return to fixed-supply factors: Generalizing from this example, we see that the return to any factor of production that is fixed in supply is economic rent.
- A factor fixed in supply has a perfectly inelastic supply curve (Key 38). Such a supply does not respond to changes in demand: supply is the same at any price.
- Thus, the payment to a fixed-supply factor is an economic rent, since any payment at all is enough to put it into use. The classic example is *land* (see Key 98).
- Joe is "fixed" in supply in that he is unique. Baseball teams cannot pay any firm to produce more "Joes." However, Joe, being human, can be put to other uses than baseball, so *all* of his baseball salary is not rent.

Key 98   Ricardo's theory of land rent

OVERVIEW *David Ricardo, an early 19th century British economist, was the first to recognize the concept of economic rent. He applied it in his theory of land rent, which shows that markets will pay economic rent to some factors of production.*

Land rent theory: Ricardo's theory assumes that farmers lease the land they use from landowners and that there are various grades of land. (Rental of land in agriculture and in urban nonresidential use is quite common today as well.)

- Assume three grades of land. Upon each, the *same* amount of other inputs (labor, equipment, seed, normal profit to the farmer-entrepreneur, etc.) is used: this amount of other inputs costs $120 per acre of land in use.
- With $120 worth of other inputs being used, an acre of "bad" land produces 50 bushels of wheat (Q_S); an acre of "good" land produces 70 bushels; an acre of "best" land yields 80 bushels.

		$P_W = \$2$		$P_W = \$3$	
Land	Q_S	TR	Rent	TR	Rent
Bad	50	100	0	150	30
Good	70	140	20	210	90
Best	80	160	40	240	120

- The wheat is sold in the market at the market price P_W. Total revenue (*TR*) per acre then is P_W multiplied by Q_S for each grade of land. In the table, when P_W is $2 per bushel, *TR* is $100, $140, and $160 for bad, good and best land, respectively.
- Each acre of land has to bring in at least $120 in order to pay the other factors of production. If *TR* is higher than $120, then the landowner gets to keep the excess. This is *rent*.
- In this example, land rent per acre is calculated as *TR* – $120.
- When P_W is $2, "bad" land would have *TR* of only $100, not enough even to pay the other inputs. Therefore, "bad" land won't be used, and its rent is 0. *TR* of good and best land exceeds the $120 needed for other inputs, resulting in rents of $20 per acre for good land and $40 per acre for best land.

Changes in product price: Regardless of the price (P_W) of the product, it still costs $120 per acre for the use of other inputs. Therefore, changes in *TR* brought on by changes in P_W will be reflected entirely in changes in land rent.

- If P_W rises to $3 per bushel, as shown in the table, *TR* will rise to $150, $210, and $240 for bad, good, and best land, respectively.
- Note that the *TR* for "bad" land now can provide the $120 needed for other inputs, so the increase in the price of wheat has brought this lesser-quality land into production.
- Rent still is *TR* − $120 per acre. It now is $30, $90, and $120 per acre for bad, good, and best land, respectively.

Fixed supply and rent: Land is a very special kind of commodity, and it is its special characteristics which make for the results shown in Ricardo's model.

- Land is fixed in supply; its supply curve is always perfectly inelastic (Key 38). Short run or long run, it is neither produced nor used up; it simply is there. As a result, it is available for use whether or not any payment is made for it. The payment received for its use, then, is *pure rent*.
- Other inputs may be fixed in supply in the short run, but in the long run they can be produced or used up; their long-run supply curves are not perfectly inelastic. In the short run, payment for such inputs may be, at least in part, rent. But in the long run it is not.

Henry George's single tax: In the late 19th century economist Henry George, following up on Ricardo's theory, suggested that all other taxes be abolished and replaced with a *single tax* upon land rent.

- He observed that most taxes have some distorting effect upon markets (Key 108). However, since supply of land is perfectly inelastic, a tax on land rent would have no effect upon the supply of land in the market. (Even if nearly all the landowner's rent is taxed away, he/she is better off renting out the land than holding it off the market and receiving nothing.)
- George also noted that at that time there appeared to be enough potentially taxable land rent in the economy to replace completely all other taxes then in use.
- Although his ideas had theoretical merit, they never got put into much practical use. Landowners had more than enough political clout to forestall any implementation of them.

Theme 11 NONMARKET ALLOCATION, GOVERNMENT, AND PUBLIC CHOICE

*M*arket failure occurs when market forces are unable, by themselves, to bring about efficient allocation of resources. Public goods are goods that cannot be efficiently allocated by markets because exclusivity of consumption and withholding from nonbuyers are impossible; government must provide such goods. Externalities represent another common kind of market failure that is sometimes redressed by government. Government also chooses to allocate some resources and to control the production of some goods itself, using nonprice allocation.

Key 99 Market failure

OVERVIEW *Market failure occurs whenever normal market forces cannot achieve the most efficient allocation of resources.*

Market failure: Competitive markets are supposed to allocate resources efficiently: the most valuable composition of total output for a given resource cost (Theme 8). However, there are some situations, or kinds of goods, for which markets cannot achieve an efficient allocation of resources.

Imperfect competition: In Theme 9 it is shown that imperfect competition does not allocate resources efficiently. Even so, there are situations when imperfect competition still has the potential to do so better than competitive markets (*natural monopoly*, Key 110). Also, government has passed considerable legislation aimed at eliminating or controlling the most damaging effects of imperfect competition (Keys 104, 105, 106).

Externalities: *Externalities* (Key 100) exist whenever all the social costs or benefits of production are not imposed upon the firm, or accrued to the firm, by the market. Externalities can be positive (beneficial) or negative (detrimental).

Public goods: *Public goods* (Key 102) are goods that by their nature cannot be allocated by the market. Sometimes they also are called *collective goods*. Specifically, they are goods that, if they are made available to anyone, become equally available to everyone (or at least to a great many others). Typical examples are many of the goods that government normally provides: roads, police protection, national defense, etc.

Economic rent: While not a blatant example of market failure, *economic rent* (Key 97) does represent a form of market failure. Specifically, *rent*, to economists, is the portion of the payment to a factor of production which *exceeds* the minimum amount that would have brought that factor into use.

Key 100 Externalities

OVERVIEW *Externalities are costs and benefits of economic activity that do not enter into the firm's own calculations of costs or revenues. Thus, in the absence of some sort of nonmarket correction (usually government action), they lead to inefficient allocation of resources.*

Externalities: Detrimental externalities impose costs on others outside the firm but do not cost the firm anything. Beneficial externalities create benefits outside the firm but provide no revenue to the firm.

Detrimental (negative) externalities: A typical example of a detrimental, or negative, externality is pollution.
- A firm's production process may send smoke into the air. The firm sustains no cost to "use" the air this way. It actually is cheaper for the firm to do so than to make the effort, and pay the expense, to clean up its exhaust.
- The surrounding area, however, sustains the cost of enduring, and cleaning up after, the effects of the firm's smoke. Therefore, there is a cost of this pollution, but it is not paid by the polluting firm; it is imposed on someone else (neighbors).

Social and private cost: The *social cost* of the polluting firm's production is the sum of its *internal costs* (private costs, which the market imposes on the firm) and the *external social costs* imposed on others by its pollution.
- One way or another, society at large has to pay the full social cost in order for the firm's production to occur. The market provides no reliable way to force the firm to pay anything but the private cost portion of total social cost, because there are no private property rights to the air.
- The cost of the detrimental externality is not necessarily imposed by the market upon the firm's customers, either. They, too, may benefit from the firm's lower costs.
- If the total social cost *could* be imposed upon the firm, its costs would be higher and its cost curves would rise. The result would be lower output, at a higher price, reflecting the true social cost of the output.

Beneficial (positive) externalities: Beneficial, or positive externalities are positive effects upon others due to private economic activity. *Example:* A flower farm exists for the purpose of making a profit by growing and selling flowers. However, it also is a very attractive thing to see and smell and so produces *positive externalities* for its neighbors and passersby.

- The market does not provide the firm (flower farm) any way to collect the extra value to society of the beneficial externality, even though the firm is responsible for producing it.
- If the firm could collect the value of the beneficial externalities it produces, its perceived demand and marginal revenue (Key 69) would increase and it would produce more.

Externalities and efficiency: Externalities are an example of market failure: social costs and benefits are not the same as the firm's cost and revenue curves (or functions). The costs imposed by the market alone are not the actual social (or "real") costs.

- *Negative externalities:* the market doesn't take into account the portion of the social cost not borne by the firm. The firm's costs, as imposed by the market, are less than the total social costs. Resources are misallocated; the firm produces more, and at a lower price, than is warranted by social cost.
- *Positive externalities:* the market doesn't provide the firm the full value of the social benefit it creates. The firm's revenues (benefits), as imposed by the market, are less than the total social benefits. Resources are misallocated; the firm produces less, and at a lower price, than is warranted by actual social benefit.

Remedies for externalities: The market provides no remedy for the misallocation of resources caused by externalities. Therefore, nonmarket means have to be found. The most common one is government action.

- *Government regulation*: In many areas, state and federal governments apply regulations that force some firms to "internalize" negative externalities. Significant examples are antipollution laws that require firms to pay the costs of remedying negative pollution externalities.
- *Taxation:* Government also can impose a tax upon firms creating negative externalities; the tax collections then are used to reimburse those who actually do pay these external costs. (*Problems:* accurately measuring the social cost involved; how to see to it that those who really do pay the external costs are the ones who get compensated.)
- *Subsidy:* In the case of positive externalities, government can subsidize (Key 101) firms that produce them, thus providing the firms with revenue fully reflecting the social benefit they produce.

Key 101 Nonmarket resource allocation

OVERVIEW *In an unregulated economy, price is the mechanism that allocates resources and determines what, and how much of it, will be produced. However, most of the world's economies include some level of government regulation and influence. Some of this influence is designed to allocate resources in ways different from the way in which the price system would.*

Nonprice allocation: The price system, as implemented in the market, is supposed to be the means of effecting efficient distribution of resources. Sometimes, however, the market doesn't do so (Key 99). Some resources, therefore, are allocated in ways that do not rely upon the market.
- Some resources, such as talent, red hair, athletic skill, and intelligence, are allocated by nature (genetics). You either have them (in varying degrees) or you don't, and no system, economic or otherwise, can redistribute them.
- Public goods (Key 102) by their very nature cannot be allocated efficiently by a market-price system. Usually government ends up controlling their production, distribution, and use. Remedies for other forms of market failure, if they are to be implemented at all, also are effected by government.

Government and the market: Government *redistributes* resources by collecting taxes and spending or paying the money to persons different from those who paid the taxes. *Examples:* social security and medicare. Sometimes government also steps into a price-driven market for the express purpose of changing the manner in which its goods and/or inputs are distributed or priced.

Rationing: Rationing usually occurs when, for some reason, there is a considerable reduction of supply of goods considered necessary or desirable by public policy. During World War II production of many consumer goods was curtailed because the government deliberately redirected resources into military production. Supply of these goods shifted inward greatly.
- Left to itself, the market would have reached equilibrium at much higher prices, with much lower quantity supplied.
- A *rationing* system redistributed these goods among the entire population, not just those who could afford the higher prices.

To buy these goods consumers needed not only money but *ration coupons* distributed by government.

- Rationing often is accompanied by *price controls*.

Price and market controls: *Price controls* limit the extent by which prices can rise or fall in particular markets. Marketing controls limit the supply that firms can provide in the market. Price controls were used in World War II to prevent *profiteering* (gaining "excessive" profits) by producers of goods that were in very limited supply.

- Until the deregulatory days of the 1980s, federal price controls applied to industries such as transportation and banking. During the 1940s many localities imposed rent controls; some (notably in New York City) still exist.
- The U.S. government still uses some marketing controls in agriculture, which limit the quantities suppliers may bring to market (and so keep prices higher).

Black markets: The price system is powerful; when government tries to overcome it, *black markets* often appear. Black markets are illegal price-driven markets that exist to get around government controls.

- When rationing is imposed, underground markets for ration coupons often appear. Consumers receiving coupons can use them to buy the rationed goods or sell the coupons and do without the goods. While this does not distribute the goods the way the government wants, it does *redistribute income:* buyers of coupons pay the true market price for the goods, but instead of producers receiving the full price, part of it is paid to those who sell their coupons.
- In areas with rent control, new tenants may pay very high "key deposits" in order to occupy the inexpensive rent-controlled dwelling. They pay closer to a true market price, but part of the price is disguised as something else.

Subsidy: *Subsidy* occurs when government makes direct or indirect (such as tax breaks) payments in order to encourage certain forms of production and/or consumption.

- Producers are subsidized in order to encourage them to produce in certain ways, and to reduce their costs. The effect of a subsidy is to shift the supply curve downward, since subsidized suppliers no longer have to cover all their costs from the revenues they receive from selling their goods.
- Consumers can be subsidized as well. The tax-deductibility of home mortgage interest but not of rent payments encourages home ownership. Subsidies to low-income groups (welfare, food stamps, etc.) are supposed to encourage a certain minimum level of subsistence.

Key 102 Public goods

OVERVIEW *Public goods, also called collective goods, are goods that cannot be allocated efficiently by market forces. Their nature is such that if they are made available to anyone, they become available to everyone.*

Public goods: Some goods cannot be allocated efficiently by markets because their consumption cannot be made *exclusive*. Such goods are called *public goods*, or *collective goods*.
- A public good is consumed *collectively*. Makng it available to *anyone* automatically makes it available to *everyone* (or, at least, very many others).
- Private goods can be *withheld* if no payment is made—if you don't pay for it, you don't get it. Also, consumption of private goods is *exclusive*—if I buy something, it's mine and I get to enjoy it all to myself.
- Public goods cannot be withheld from nonpayers. Further, consumption of a public good cannot be made exclusive only to those who will pay for it. One person's consumption of, or benefit from, a public good does not reduce anyone else's consumption or benefit.
- Examples of public goods are many of the things provided by government: police and fire protection, national defense, etc.
- For goods such as these, if they are provided at all, they benefit everyone. It is all but impossible, for example, to provide the protection of national defense privately. In order to protect adequately those who would "buy" it, protection has to be extended to everyone, and there is no way to keep "nonbuyers" from benefiting from it.

Demand for public goods: There is no doubt that public goods are desirable and that consumers "want" them and should be willing to pay some price to have them.
- However, the rational thing for consumers to do is not to express a willingness to buy such goods. So long as *anyone* else pays for it, all consumers will receive it. In the same vein, any consumer who pays for such a good is making a free gift to everyone else.
- Therefore, the rational thing for the *economic man* (Key 12) to do is to wait for *someone else* to bear the cost. Such a situation cannot be solved efficiently by market forces.

Key 103 Public goods: Costs and benefits

OVERVIEW *Public goods cannot be supplied by firms operating in conventional markets because there is no way for the firms to enforce exclusivity or withhold supply from nonpayers. Government is the significant supplier and usually uses measurement of costs and benefits to determine what, and how much, to provide.*

Supply of public goods: Government is the usual provider of public goods (Key 102). Through taxation, it can *enforce* payment by those who benefit from the supply of such goods. The exclusivity problem doesn't matter since it serves the entire society.
- Problems still arise in determining the optimal amounts (supply) of public goods to be provided, since there is no way for the market to determine the efficient level of supply.
- Government therefore uses *nonmarket* means of allocating resources to the production of public goods. These, often, are noneconomic: political, social, etc.
- Also, there is no economic way to allocate the cost of public goods among taxpayers in proportion to the benefits received by each one. Tax policy includes noneconomic criteria, such as "fairness," ability to pay, ease of identification, and collection.

Costs-benefit analysis: One method used to determine the kind, allocation, and quantity of public goods (and sometimes the taxation methods used to pay for them) is to analyze the *social costs and benefits* of producing and distributing them.
- Social costs are the actual dollar costs of providing the public good, plus any costs imposed by externalities (Key 100).
- Social benefits are the external benefits provided by the public good. Since nobody directly pays for them, their advantages (benefits) to the society have to be measured as externalities.
- Once social costs and benefits have been determined, they are compared. If benefits exceed costs, it is worthwhile to provide the public good in question, because the population as a group receives more from the good than they pay to get it. Likewise, if costs exceed benefits, the public good should not be provided.
- Cost-benefit analysis has problems, most notably in the accurate *measurement* of costs and benefits (Key 104).

Key 104 Measuring costs and benefits

OVERVIEW *While cost-benefit analysis looks good on paper, in the real world serious difficulties are encountered in identifying costs and benefits and setting a value upon them.*

Measurement problems: Cost-benefit analysis (Key 103) is meant to substitute for the automatic determination of costs, benefits, and allocation that markets normally provide. There are two key problems inherent in it: (a) identifying *all* the costs and benefits involved, and (b) determining a *dollar value* of *each* of them.

- *Direct costs* and benefits are easiest to identify measure. Direct costs are the actual costs of production of the public good. Direct benefits are obvious and immediate savings to government, firms, and consumers.
- *External (indirect)* costs and benefits are harder to identify and even harder to measure. Many are subjective: people get pleasure from a new park; people dislike having a new highway near their homes. How do you put a value on these?
- *Future* costs and benefits. Many public goods are like capital goods: They last a long time and provide benefits (and some costs) far into the future (roads, dams, parks, etc.). Setting a *present value* on future costs and benefits is necessarily "iffy." This involves forecasting the future, which never can be done with certainty.

Example: Existing roads in a certain area are congested and unsafe. The government considers building a new superhighway to handle much of the traffic load.

- Direct costs include land, construction, future maintenance, etc. External costs include local auto pollution, dislocation of homes and businesses to make way for the road, losses to remaining businesses due to lower traffic, etc.
- Benefits include easing congestion on existing roads, greater efficiency in travel (saving time, saving fuel due to reduced stop-and-go driving, etc.), fewer accidents due to the safer road, less future congestion, increases in land values along the new road due to better accessibility, etc.
- Many of these costs and benefits will accrue in the future and are hard to predict accurately. Also, only a few costs and benefits are mentioned here; the actual list is almost endless. You probably can think of several more yourself.

Key 105 Public choice

OVERVIEW *Public choice refers to the manner in which government decisions with regard to resource allocation are made. Public choice economics is the study of these decisions and their relationship to the efficient allocation of resources.*

Making public choices: Earlier Keys in this Theme point out that government often makes decisions that affect the allocation of scarce resources; some also discuss the problems inherent in making such nonmarket allocative decisions.
- The objective of government usually is to make decisions reflecting public wants; this means that it needs to know what the public wants.
- *Public choice economics* uses economic analysis to explain the behavior of government.

Voting: Ideally, government makes decisions by putting questions to the people themselves, the voters.
- *Unanimity:* This very rare situation is the ideal government decision-making scenario: Everyone wants the government to do same thing; it does so, and everybody is happy.
- *Majority rule:* In the U.S., most public choice is, supposedly, made as a result of *majority rule*. This means that not everyone is satisfied with a government action (a negative *political externality*), but at least more than half of them are.
- *Plurality:* This is a situation where the chosen action is preferred not by a majority but by more voters than prefer any other alternative. A plurality can occur only when more than two choices are being voted on at the same time. (With only two alternatives, the vote must end up as a tie, or with a clear majority winner.)

Representation, bureaucracy: In today's complex societies, it is impractical to put most government decisions to public votes.
- Therefore, the public elects *representatives* who form legislatures which make the major decisions.
- Even the representatives cannot make all decisions; they set policy and guidelines, and most of the day-to-day decisions are made by *bureaucrats*. Bureaucrats are nonelected government officials who carry out specific, often very narrow tasks.

Key 106 Public choice problems

OVERVIEW *Because of its nature, public choice is beset with problems in the determination of voters' wants, and efficient allocation of resources.*

Voting problems: As it is done in the real world, voting situations often do not result in decisions that the majority of people would approve. Also, it is quite possible for a genuine majority vote not to reflect the actual costs and benefits to all voters as a group.

- *Logrolling*: This is vote-trading ("I'll vote for what you want if you vote for what I want"). Logrolling can accumulate majorities that don't reflect voters' true wishes.

- *Rational ignorance*: Voting on issues takes time and requires the voter to be informed. If a voter perceives an issue as being relatively unimportant to him/her, or if the result of the voting appears to be a foregone conclusion, the rational action would be not to acquire the information needed to vote intelligently. Voters may even ignore the election entirely. For example, George Bush won the 1988 election in a near "landslide." However, barely over 60% of eligible voters participated, so, in fact, he was elected by fewer than 40% of them.

- *Special-interest groups:* These are minorities of voters who consider certain issues very important. They spend time and effort to convince others to vote their way and are sure to cast their vote, while rational ignorance may keep many other voters from the polls.

Voter's paradox: Even without the real-life problems described above, majority-rule voting can lead to odd results. A well used example is the voter's paradox:

- Assume three voters: Joe, Sue, and Lucy. Each has his/her own set of preferences among the three policies (A, B, and C) that they are going to vote upon. ("A>B>C", etc., means "A is preferred to B, B is preferred to C", etc.):

     Joe: A>B>C   Sue: B>C>A   Lucy: C>A>B

- The policies are voted upon two at a time. In the three different possible elections between two policies, the results are as follows:

     A versus B: A wins, 2 to 1   (Joe, Lucy for A; Sue for B)
     B versus C: B wins, 2 to 1   (Joe, Sue for B; Lucy for C)
     A versus C: C wins, 2 to 1   (Sue, Lucy for C; Joe for A)

- If voters prefer A to B and they also prefer B to C, you would expect them to prefer A to C. But in this situation, C wins an election between A and C. This is the *voter's paradox*; it shows that it is possible for majority rule to lead to an "illogical" result.

The median voter: This is the person who is directly in the middle on a particular issue. If the issue is public expenditure, exactly half the voters want more to be spent than the median voter does, and exactly half want less to be spent.
- The median voter, therefore, is the "tiebreaker": the one whose vote actually determines the outcome.
- Note that on different issues, the median voter will be a different person. Also, the median voter usually doesn't have enough information to know that he/she is "the one."

Problems with majority rule: Even without logrolling, special interests, and the other problems mentioned, majority rule can lead to economically inefficient results or to other problems that are difficult to resolve.
- *Individual wants*: Majority rule doesn't respond to the wants of all individuals; in any vote, the minority will be dissatisfied.
- *Intensity of wants*: How intensely *nonmedian* voters feel about an issue has no bearing upon the outcome. A vote may be decided by a majority who care only slightly about the outcome while some members of the minority may have cared very intensely. Contrast this with the market system where preference, and its intensity, translates directly into willingness (or unwillingness) to pay.
- *Yes-no questions:* Many elections are "yes-no" votes on a single approach chosen from many possibilities (usually as a result of log rolling, special-interest influence, etc.). Actually, it may not be the preferred choice of many voters. However, when faced with an all-or-nothing choice, many voters may prefer it to the only other choice available: nothing at all.

Politics: A central problem of public choice is that the benefits of many government policies are concentrated while their costs are spread thinly and not easy to identify. Politicians can appeal to various special-interest groups and get their votes, knowing that most voters will be unable to tell how much such pandering actually is costing them. The result is that special interests often can elect politicians who will see to it that their interests are served, even though doing so is clearly economically inefficient.

Theme 12 GOVERNMENT: TAXATION AND REGULATION

*G*overnment affects microeconomic entities in several ways. Imposition of taxes distorts demand and supply. Government also directly regulates some industries and firms.

Key 107 Taxation

OVERVIEW *Government acquires most of the money it spends by imposing taxes within the economy. There are many different kinds of taxes. Taxation necessarily affects markets and their equilibrium prices and quantities. Some broad-based taxes can affect many markets at once.*

Taxes: Government collects taxes to obtain revenue, part of which is used to provide public goods. Many taxes exist just to generate revenue and don't necessarily reflect the quantity of public goods and government services received by those paying the tax. Other taxes are earmarked for certain purposes that are supposed to benefit the payers.

- *Income taxes* are imposed upon the incomes of firms and consumers.
- *Sales taxes* are percentage taxes upon some (but not all) purchases of goods and services. Some sales taxes, especially at the local level, may be earmarked to pay for certain things.
- An *excise* tax is a specific cash amount applied to each unit of the taxed good. *Examples:* taxes on cigarettes, alcohol, "gas guzzler" tax on some autos. Some excise taxes are *earmarked;* for example, the federal tax on gasoline pays for highways.
- *Progressivity* of a tax refers to the relationship between the taxpayer's level of income and the portion of income taken by the tax. A *progressive* tax (such as federal income tax) takes a larger portion of higher incomes than of lower. A *regressive* tax (such as most sales taxes) takes a larger proportion of lower incomes than of higher ones.

Effects of taxes upon markets: Taxes necessarily alter (distort) normal market equilibrium, since they can affect costs and incomes. Excise taxes are discussed in Key 108.

- A sales tax raises the supply curve as an excise tax does. (However, since a sales tax is a percentage amount of market price, S and ST, as shown in the graph in Key 108, diverge (move farther apart) as quantity supplied increases.)
- An income tax imposed on consumers has the effect of reducing consumers' spendable income and shifts the demand curve inward (Key 28). An income tax upon firms shifts the supply curve outward (Key 29) as it increases costs. So do *privilege taxes, license fees,* etc.

Key 108 Tax incidence

(excise tax example)

OVERVIEW *Tax incidence refers to the manner in which the actual payment of a tax is "shared" between suppliers (firms) and consumers of the taxed good. The most common example of tax incidence used in microeconomics courses is that of an excise tax. The incidence of a tax in any particular market depends upon the type of tax that it is and the respective elasticities of supply and demand in that market.*

Excise tax example: In the graph, demand is *DD*. *Before the tax is imposed,* supply is *S*, equilibrium price (Key 25) is P_E, and equilibrium quantity supplied is Q_E.

- Imposing the excise tax adds the amount of the tax to the firm's cost: a constant amount per unit produced. Though the supplier usually collects the tax (by adding it to price), it is paid directly to government and does not increase the supplier's revenue.
- The supply curve rises vertically by the full amount of the tax, from *S* to supply curve S_T; the market's suppliers simply add the amount of the tax to the price at all levels of quantity supplied. A new equilibrium occurs at E_T, with a lower quantity supplied of Q_T.

KEY GRAPH

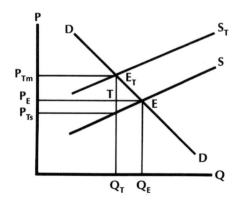

Incidence of the excise tax: When the tax is imposed, two prices are viewed in the market. Consumers pay price P_{Tm}, the equilibrium price set by DD and S_T. Suppliers, however, "receive" a lower "price": P_{Ts}. The difference $(P_{Tm} - P_{Ts})$ between the two prices is the amount of the tax. Consumers pay it, but suppliers don't get to keep it because government takes it.

- The *incidence* (sometimes called *tax burden*) of the tax is the distribution of the "payment" of the tax among consumers and suppliers.
- Incidence upon consumers is the amount by which market price increases over P_E when the tax is imposed: $(P_{Tm} - P_E)$. Incidence upon suppliers is the amount by which the net price they receive (after the tax is paid) falls short of P_E: $(P_E - P_{Ts})$.
- The total of the two incidence amounts is the amount of the tax.

Elasticity and tax incidence: The incidence of a tax in any market depends upon elasticities of supply and demand in that market.

- The more inelastic demand is relative to supply, the more the tax will impact upon consumers and the less will be the drop in quantity supplied. The more inelastic supply is relative to demand, the more the tax incidence will be upon suppliers and the less will be the drop in quantity supplied.
- The graph shows the effects of imposing an excise tax. When demand is inelastic, consumers spend more of their incomes on the good after the tax is imposed. If demand is elastic, imposing the tax will lead to a lower *TR* being spent on the good.
- With a ruler, draw different *SS* and *DD* curves through point *E* to demonstrate the effects of various elasticities.

Key 109 Collusion and antitrust laws

OVERVIEW *Antitrust laws first came into being in the U.S. late in the 19th century, in response to monopoly and collusion in emerging heavy industry. Since then, antitrust action and legislation has been refined. Its objective is to prohibit the "restraint of trade" and to encourage competition; the economic objective is to reduce monopoly profits and encourage more efficient (lower-cost) production.*

History of antitrust legislation: Collusion and monopolistic practices in heavy industry in the late 19th century created situations in which monopoly profit and control of markets were obvious. Federal antitrust legislation since that time has endeavored to regulate and/or prevent such activity.

- Congress created the *Interstate Commerce Commission* in 1887 to regulate railroads.
- The *Sherman Act* (1890) was the first attempt to control monopoly and collusion. It declared monopoly and "trade restraint" (overt price fixing) to be illegal.
- The *Clayton Act* of 1914 further extended antitrust law to additional activities that lessened competition. It made tying contracts (requiring a customer to buy one product as a condition of acquiring another) illegal, prohibited overt price discrimination (Key 86), and banned mergers that would lessen competition.
- Congress also created the *Federal Trade Commission* in 1914; it is empowered to investigate the conduct of businesses in interstate commerce, to seek out unfair competition.
- The *Celler-Kefauver Act* (1950) extended the power of the Federal Government to control trade-restraining activity. It also closed loopholes in antitrust law.
- Penalties for violation of antitrust legislation also have become more severe over time.

Arguments favoring antitrust enforcement: Perhaps the most significant arguments supporting antitrust enforcement can be found in basic economic theory: monopoly and oligopoly produce excess profits and are inherently inefficient (do not produce output at the lowest possible cost).

- Price-fixing and collusion, illegal under antitrust law, serve no purpose other than to increase profits of the conspiring firms. These activities increase costs, with no corresponding social benefit. Outlawing such practices encourages more efficient production.
- Antitrust law bans unfair and deceptive practice, which can interfere with the knowledge that consumers need in order to make rational economic decisions.
- "Trust-busting" (breaking up large monopolies) often has had very successful outcomes by increasing competition.

Arguments against antitrust enforcement: Major arguments against antitrust enforcement concentrate upon what might be termed excessive zeal on the part of enforcement: bigness is not necessarily badness.

- It can be a penalty for success. A firm can be so efficient that it comes to dominate a market simply because its product is better and/or cheaper than anything its competitors can make. Regulating such a firm or forcing it to give up part of its market so as to enhance competition actually can be counterproductive.
- Modern international markets favor the large, integrated company or industry. Some other countries (notably Japan) have governments that very actively support their large industries and firms, rather than hounding them about their excessive size or market domination.

Key 110 Regulation of natural monopoly

OVERVIEW *Natural monopolies are industries in which economies of scale are so significant that larger firms, no matter how big, always will have lower average costs than smaller ones. Many such natural monopolies are allowed to exist, but only because direct government regulation limits their profits and forces them to produce more efficiently than they otherwise would.*

Natural monopoly: A natural monopoly is any industry in which economies of scale persist so much that increasing the size of the firm always leads to lower long-run average costs.
- The obvious examples are such firms as utility companies and railroads. These require very heavy expenditure upon capital equipment.
- They can be efficient as monopolies because it is obviously unproductive to have two competing railroads side by side or two sets of gas or electric lines on the same street, etc.

KEY GRAPH

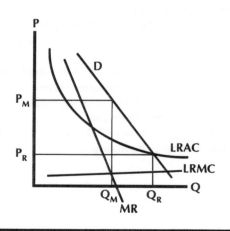

Graphical representation of natural monopoly: The firm's inclination, of course, is to produce where $MR = MC$ (Key 77). However, government regulation attempts, instead, to require the firm to produce on its long run average cost curve (Key 62) where $D = LRAC$.

- The firm normally will produce where $MR = MC$; in the graph, that is output Q_M, at price P_M. This will lead to considerable monopoly profits, since P_M is well above MC (Key 78).
- Government recognizes that the natural monopoly can be the most efficient means of producing in this market and so allows the natural monopoly to continue to exist. However, government will regulate the firm so as to produce more output at a lower price than the free-market equilibrium.
- Virtually all utility companies (electricity, telephone, water, natural gas) are regulated by state and federal governments. Some (usually local) governments bypass the regulation of a private firm by owning utility services themselves (most commonly water and sewage). The transportation industry (railroads, airlines, trucking, etc.) is regulated to some degree by the U.S. government.

Effects of government regulation: Government attempts to require, through regulation, that the firm produce where $D = LRAC$.
- Because of the continuing economies of scale that characterize a natural monopoly, $LRAC$ is always falling. Therefore, long-run marginal cost ($LRMC$) must be *below LRAC*: MC always intersects ATC from below at the low point on ATC (Key 61). Since $LRAC$ is still falling, the low point of $LRAC$ hasn't been reached, and $LRMC$ must be lower still.
- If government requires the firm to produce where $LRMC$ is equal to price (intersection of $LRMC$ and D), the firm will lose money. A price set at $LRMC$ would be below $LRAC$ and the firm would suffer losses, *even though such a price would be allocatively efficient.*
- By requiring the firm to produce at the point where price equals $LRAC$, the government eliminates excess profit. The firm still earns its normal profit (Key 16) or, as regulators put it, a *reasonable rate of return on investment.*
- At this point, price is lower (P_R) and output higher (Q_R) than at free-market monopoly equilibrium.

Key 111 Regulation, deregulation, reregulation

OVERVIEW *During the first half of the 20th century, several industries came under government regulation to one degree or another. Since the late 1970s there has been a trend to reduce regulation; it has met with mixed success.*

The case for deregulation: By the late 1970s there was considerable (but not unanimous) agreement among economists and politicians that some elements of regulation were unproductive. Especially at the federal level, this led to a program of *deregulation*: reducing or eliminating government regulation of some industries. The idea was that deregulation would improve competitive effects and thereby lead to greater output at lower prices.

- Some regulated industries really weren't natural monopolies (Key 110); the trucking industry is an example. Regulation of them was more the result of political than economic decisions.
- Some industries found regulation *advantageous*. Competition was kept at a minimum. Influence by the industry upon friendly legislatures and regulatory agencies could be relied upon to assure that profits would remain desirably high.
- In some industries, it appeared that regulation actually fostered lower output and higher prices than might exist in a more competitive market (airlines and trucking are examples).
- Technological advances in some industries have made possible more viable competition (telecommunications is an example).

Effects of deregulation: The deregulation effort of the 1980s has had various outcomes. Some examples:

- *Success:* It appears that deregulation of interstate trucking has led, for the most part, to increased competition and lower prices.
- *Mixed results*: Deregulation of the domestic petroleum industry has led to more reliable supplies, but at higher prices in many situations. Deregulation of the airline industry is said to have led to lower overall fares. However, several airlines failed after deregulation, which has led to greater oligopolistic concentration. Also, it appears that many cities now are being "monopolized" by a single dominant airline.

- *Failure*: Within a decade after serious deregulation of the savings and loan industry began, much of the industry collapsed, at an astronomical cost to the federal government. Expansion into unfamiliar business areas and taking greater than previously allowed risk appear to be the main causes. However, some economists argue that the industry was too sick to survive even before deregulation took effect. In the mid-1980s federal legislation banned local regulation of cable TV systems. Since then average rates have increased twice as fast as general inflation, even after accounting for improvements in service. Some economists argue that these increases simply make up for unrealistically low rates imposed before deregulation; others argue that cable companies wouldn't have gone into business in regulated areas unless the then-regulated rates were already profitable.

Existing regulation: In spite of an era of deregulation, plenty of economic activity still is regulated or prohibited by various governments. Much of the regulation of utility companies is still in place. A lot of existing regulation has a noneconomic basis. "Moral" regulation is an example; it leads to restrictions, in some places but not in others, upon gambling, prostitution, sales of alcohol, nude beaches, etc.

Reregulation: At present there appears to be a growing national sentiment for some increase in the amount of regulation, even from some of the industries themselves. Deregulation has led to some unexpected results, not all of which are desirable (see above). Also, perceived abuses in currently unregulated industries (credit reporting is an example) encourage sentiment for additional regulation.

GLOSSARY

average total cost
(AC) The mean cost per unit of output. Total cost divided by total output: TC/Q.

ceteris paribus
Latin for "all else being equal"; a fundamental assumption in many economic models.

change in demand
A movement of the demand curve to a different location, resulting in different quantities demanded in the market at every price.

change in supply
A movement of the supply curve to a different location, resulting in different quantities supplied in the market at every price.

demand
The quantity of a good or service that consumers are prepared to purchase at a given time, under given circumstances.

demand curve
In a graph, depiction of the quantities of a good that will be demanded at each possible price.

diseconomies
Increases in average and total costs due to larger firm size; occurs on the portion of the long-run average cost curve ($LRAC$) that is upward-sloping.

economics
The study of how society allocates scarce resources.

economies of scale
Increases in average and total costs due to larger firm size; occurs on the portion of the long-run average cost curve (LRAC) that is downward-sloping.

elastic demand
The portion of a demand curve in which the percent change in price is less than the percent change in quantity demanded.

elasticity
For supply or demand curves, the ratio of the percent change in quantity supplied/demanded to the percent change in the price of the good.

equilibrium   The state in which there are no market forces that will cause a firm to change its output, a household to change its consumption pattern, or a market to effect any changes in price or quantity supplied.

factor of production   *see Inputs.*

fixed cost (FC)   The costs that a firm must incur regardless of the quantity of its output.

indifference curve   A curve showing the various combinations of goods that yield the household the same total utility (the household is *indifferent* to distinctions among these combinations).

indifference map   A graph showing all of the indifference curves (each representing a different level of total utility) of a household.

inelastic demand   The portion of a demand curve in which the percent change in price exceeds the percent change in quantity demanded.

inferior good   A good for which quantity demanded falls as household income increases or as its price increases, because households substitute a better quality or otherwise more desirable, and more expensive, good for it.

inputs   The goods and services (land, labor, capital, raw materials) that firms must buy in order to use them to produce output.

law of demand   The result in economic theory that states (for normal goods) that as price falls, quantity demanded increases and vice versa (*ceteris paribus*).

law of supply   The result in economic theory that states (for normal goods) that as price falls, quantity supplied decreases and vice versa (*ceteris paribus*).

long run   In the theory of the firm, the time period during which all costs become variable and there are no fixed costs.

long run average cost curve (*LRAC*)	The curve that shows the firm's average costs in the long run; it "envelopes" all of the firm's short-run average cost curves.
macroeconomics	The study of the economy as a whole, examining inflation, interest rates, money supply, investment, government (taxation and spending), and economy-wide output.
marginal cost (*MC*)	The costs sustained by the firm due to the production of one additional unit of output.
marginal factor cost (*MFC*)	The additional cost to the firm of employing or using one additional unit of an input.
marginal physical product (*MRP*)	The output obtained by the firm from using one additional unit of an input.
marginal revenue (*MR*)	The revenue received by the firm from selling one additional unit of output in the market.
marginal revenue product (*MRP*)	The revenue received by the firm from selling, in the market, the additional output produced by the use of a marginal unit of an input.
marginal utility (*MU*)	The utility received by a consumer from the consumption of one additional unit of a good.
microeconomics	The study of the actions of the individual elements in the economy (firms and households) which determine the equilibrium levels of the production of goods and services.
market	The economic arena in which all goods and services are exchanged (bought and sold) and in which equilibrium prices and quantities supplied are determined.
model	A theoretical representation of a real-world phenomenon, usually simplified in order to make its examination easier.
monopolistic competition	A market in which there are many firms, a differentiated product, and easy entry.

monopoly   A market in which a single firm produces the entire quantity supplied and entry of new firms is impossible.

normal good   A good for which the consumer's demand increases as the consumer's income increases.

oligopoly   A market with few firms, dominated by a single (or very few) large firms; product differentiation may exist, but it is not necessary.

opportunity cost   When taking a particular action, the loss of the value of the next best action.

output   The quantity of a good or service that a firm makes available in the market.

perfect competition   A market in which there are many firms, none of which is large enough to affect the market by itself; product is undifferentiated, perfect knowledge exists, $MR = P$; and there is easy entry.

price   The money measure of the value which must be exchanged in the market to acquire a unit of a good or service.

price leadership   A market in which there are few firms and a dominant firm's pricing behavior is followed by the smaller firms in the market.

profit maximization   The objective of the firm; it occurs when the firm produces the quantity for which marginal revenue and marginal cost are equal ($MR = MC$).

public good   A good for which normal market characteristics of exclusivity and exclusion do not apply; if it is supplied at all, it is supplied to everyone whether or not he/she pays for it.

quantity demanded   The quantity of a good or service that consumers in the market will buy at a given price.

quantity supplied   The quantity of a good or service that firms will produce at a given price.

scarce resource   Any economic good or service that does not exist in large enough quantity for all people to have all they want at a zero price.

short run   In the theory of the firm, a span of time during which at least one input is fixed.

supply   Willingness and ability of firms to produce goods and services and make them available in the market.

tax incidence   The manner in which the burden of paying a tax falls upon those who are affected by it.

total cost (TC)   The sum of fixed cost and variable cost.

total revenue (TR)   The total sum of money, at a given price, spent on a good in the market by consumers and received by firms.

total utility (TU)   The sum of the utility received by a household from all the goods and services upon which it spends its income.

utility   The "usefulness," or satisfaction, that consumers get from consuming goods and services.

utility maximization   The objective of the household as it determines its consumption pattern—to obtain the highest utility possible within the limits of its income.

variable cost (VC)   The firm's cost for those inputs whose quantities used vary as output varies.

INDEX